PENGUIN BUSINESS

TINY RICE GRAINS

Lyn Lee, an influential figure in the diversity, equity, and inclusion (DEI) space, brings a wealth of experience and a uniquely Asian perspective to her debut book, *Tiny Rice Grains*.

She is the first Asian woman to be appointed as Shell's Global Chief DE&I Officer in 2018 and remained in position till her early retirement in December 2024.

Under Lyn's leadership and vision for DEI, Shell has received numerous awards, including the Cannes Corporate Media & TV Awards and EVCOM Clarion GOLD Award for its DEI engagement and communications strategy; the Brandon Hall DEI GOLD Award for Best Advance in Leadership Development for Women and Best Use of AI to Improve Diversity, Equity, Inclusion and Belonging Programmes.

She also serves as the chairwoman of the board of advisers for the School of Humanities & Interdisciplinary Studies at Ngee Ann Polytechnic, Singapore.

When not championing DEI initiatives, the mother of two daughters loves the thrill of hiking through unchartered territories and was a travel concierge for Bhutan. The WSET (Wine and Spirits Education Trust)-certified woman enjoys learning about wines and making new friends.

Tiny Rice Grains

How Small and Impactful Actions Build Inclusive Workplaces

Lyn R. Lee

BUSINESS

An imprint of Penguin Random House

PENGUIN BUSINESS

Penguin Business is an imprint of the Penguin Random House group of companies whose addresses can be found at global.penguinrandomhouse.com

Published by Penguin Random House SEA Pte Ltd
40 Penjuru Lane, #03-12, Block 2
Singapore 609216

First published in Penguin Business by Penguin Random House SEA 2025

10 9 8 7 6 5 4 3 2 1

ISBN 9789815280913

Typeset in Garamond by MAP Systems, Bangalore, India

www.penguin.sg

Dedicated to my late mother, Mary Phek-Kee, who taught me so much through her storytelling, all of which had a teachable moment, and always brought home the point that being right is less important, but doing the right thing is the most important. Mum had a way of making her stories personal, and as a child, I remember looking forward to sitting next to Mum by her sewing machine as she spun tales as effortlessly as the thread. Mum also role-modelled what it meant to be an empowered individual, who took decisive action for the betterment of herself and those within her sphere of influence. She was my pillar of strength, helping me through the most difficult periods in my life.

To my late father, Camillus Keng-Chee, for being the supportive husband to my mum, who was ahead of his time, for always being the consistent and reliable father and grandfather to me and my children.

Contents

Part 3: Caring About Humanity

Foreword

I am honoured to have been asked to write a forward to this book. Not being used to doing so, I suppose that the initial questions I asked myself were whether I would be comfortable endorsing Lyn's thinking, whether the world needs another book about diversity, equity, and inclusion, and who might benefit most from reading such a book?

The first of those questions is easily answered. I have known Lyn for many years and I can confidently attest to the effectiveness with which she has led in the DEI realm in Shell and the commensurate respect in which she has been held. Having read *Tiny Rice Grains,* I could equally easily attest to the authenticity of the thinking expressed here, which does not propose theoretical models, but is rather framed as a series of thoughtful reflections on experience. It is, therefore, a very familiar portrait of the manner in which I have seen Lyn exercise her leadership. She has never been strident, judgemental or self-righteous; on the contrary, Lyn has consistently been curious, courageous, and caring.

Do we need another book about DEI? Any potential author should first ask themselves whether they have anything new to say or, alternatively, whether they can provide a better synthesis of existing ideas and practices than previous ones. The subject is, of course, of great importance and thus worthy of further study.

I think when future generations look back at the history of the last thirty-five years (a period that encompasses both Lyn and my own careers) they are likely to judge that, along with the impact of globalization and of the digital revolution, it has been the diversification of the workforce that has shaped the greatest social change. Much has been achieved—which is a legitimate cause for both pride and optimism and this indeed is rightly an optimistic book—but much remains to be done. While some of the more obvious intellectual battles at the foot of the DEI staircase have been mostly won, successfully exploiting the full potential of DEI in the workplace is far from done, and I suggest that this poses a more subtle, nuanced, and complex challenge than the earlier stage of the journey. This is certainly the case in multinational companies that necessarily straddle a variety of social and political cultures. I think that Lyn's book is geared to prompting the questions and behaviours necessary to address that challenge sensitively and effectively.

I also think that there is much good synthesis here. Lyn has brought out the power of integrated leadership thinking and the importance of enrolling different stakeholders to enable the achievement of DEI aspired outcomes. She has illustrated the causal correlation between care and engagement, care and resilience, curiosity and learning, and how these attributes drive not only DEI achievements, but superior health and well-being, safety, and commercial outcomes. She brings out the importance of long-term investment in people and the consequent rewards. This makes the book not just of interest to Human Resource and DEI professionals but to any leader seeking to improve the performance of their organization. I would particularly recommend it to first-line team leaders who are seeking to develop their own leadership philosophy.

Lyn's final chapters seem to move us past the (relatively) more prosaic physical and mental enablers of diversity into an almost spiritual meditation on kindness and humanity. I think this gets to the very heart of why any of this matters in the first place and I can only commend it to you.

R.T.Cassidy

Ronan Cassidy

Chief human resources and corporate officer,

Shell plc, 2016-2023

Preface

DEI, or diversity, equity, and inclusion, is an ever-evolving area, with changing generations and changing conversations. It requires empathy, listening, and understanding, as well as an ability to work with the unknown.

The reason I have written this book is to share my own learnings and experiences, the uncomfortable truths I've had to face. Along the way, the most important lesson I have learned and grown from, is that people want to be heard, seen, and respected. In fact, the feeling of being included, valued, heard, seen, and respected, empowers them and gives them a platform to share and impact others. And so, in this book, I also bring in stories and perspectives from many others, widening the conversation and giving readers a chance to learn from a collective wisdom far greater than mine alone.

It is written with the frontline leader in mind. The leader who is at the cold face of managing the operational day-to-day, leading courageously, and building collaborative teams to perform at their best.

I have found that empathy and listening are the most important attributes in my DEI leader journey and through listening, I have been enriched. It is my wish to pass on some of these learnings, and my hope that it will affirm the work that other leaders do.

Explaining Diversity, Equity, and Inclusion: DEI

Throughout this book, I reference DEI. As there could be different definitions or assumptions about the terminology, I would like to explain how I will be addressing DEI.

Diversity encompasses all the ways we are different, such as race, religion, gender identity, sexual orientation, disability status, age, culture, thinking styles, and so on. Inclusion is the act of consciously and actively responding, embracing, and valuing the uniqueness of every individual, and leveraging the power of the unique whole. This involves having the courage to intervene when we see non-inclusive behaviours and actions.

Equity is fairness for all and is different from equality. It means we recognize the varied backgrounds and experiences of each individual. Levelling the playing field means taking purposeful and targeted action to ensure that everyone can achieve their best results.

Equity Versus Equality: How Is It different?

I've always been asked about the difference between equity versus equality. These concepts are sometimes confusing and

nuanced. I hope that the following examples illustrate and bring to life the distinct difference between the two and provide you with the clarity you need for your DEI journey.

I used to wonder about the classic visual representation of equity—people standing on boxes of different heights, trying to see over a fence. It always appeared one-dimensional to me, and I also thought that it could potentially create other inequalities because it did not address the root of the problem. For instance, why is there a fence to start with? And why is the fence of a certain height, such that it blocks the views of those who are shorter?

I believe equity is about understanding the issue as well as addressing different needs, not just handing out bigger boxes. It's about recognizing that we all have unique starting points and require different tools to reach the same destination.

Imagine a group of cyclists: some might need a tricycle for stability, others might benefit from wider tires better suited for a rough terrain. The goal isn't to give everyone the exact same bicycle, but to ensure each person has what they need to ride alongside the others.

True equity is about mobility, not just equal footing. It's about understanding the diverse contexts and challenges people face, and then working to close those gaps. It's a nuanced process, one that requires us to think beyond simple solutions.

So, how do we level the playing field?

We start by looking at social mobility, focusing on specific actions and supporting those with fewer opportunities.

Ultimately, it's about creating an ecosystem where everyone has a chance to succeed. That is how I differentiate 'equitable' from 'equal'. True equality may be ideal, but equity is something we can actively strive for.

Why Tiny Rice Grains?

In many parts of Asia, rice is the main staple and an unmistakable constant in almost every meal shared among family and friends. It is understated, plain even, but it is nourishing on its own, with or without other side dishes. Rice is so much part of the psyche that phrases such as 'Have you eaten [rice]?' are a form of greeting, and a question you would ask a loved one or a friend, to show that you care. There are also many types of rice to enjoy and appreciate and each has its own unique qualities and flavours—jasmine rice, basmati rice, brown rice, red rice, glutinous rice, long grain rice, short grain rice—all used to create the most exquisite of meals across many cultures in Asia and beyond. This diversity has enriched many who have come to appreciate the different cuisine and cultures that accompany these rice grains. It is also the foundation on which many deep and meaningful conversations have been exchanged and embraced.

But I am not the only one for whom tiny rice grains hold great meaning. My friend Girish K, from Chennai, shared his thoughts with me on what tiny rice grains mean in India, as well as how he connects them to DEI.

'There is a famous Tamil proverb: *Oru paanai sothukku oru soru padham.* It means, "For one big pot of boiling rice, a few grains are enough to test and tell the cooking tendency of the entire pot." The equivalent proverb in English is, "You may know the whole sack by a handful." In my mind, a person's character or the underlying thought processes or a person's nature can be understood by how inclusive they are towards various people, cultures, and ideas. I would say this trait of giving importance to DEI (a few grains of rice) is enough to measure the person's entire life value (big pot of rice), just as in the Tamil proverb.

'In our part of India—Tamil Nadu—even now grandmothers ask, "*Soru saaptiya pa*?" It translates to, "Did you eat rice?" Although that's the literal translation, there is a lot more meaning behind this question. It encompasses "How's your life going?", "Are you tired?", "Are you hungry?", and "Is everything okay with you?"

'So, a grandmother doesn't have to ask anything specifically, but with her one question she can create an instant bond of care and affection, while encouraging us to open up to her.

'People who are hungry, angry, disturbed, in a bad mood, or depressed, will usually break into tears when their grandmother asks just that question, "*Soru saaptiya pa?*" I can't find a simpler yet more impactful question than that, because food is fundamental, as is caring, lending a shoulder to cry on, hearing others' problems, creating a safe space for people to be themselves, and, above all, making them feel at home. If rice and its feeling isn't about DEI, I don't know what is.

'Being Asian, we can relate ourselves to rice more than any other food. Rice is our staple. Though we speak different languages, have different cultures, and wear different clothes across the continent, we all have rice as our main food. Though we have different side dishes (I consider language, nationality, and culture to be the side dishes in a DEI context), our main dish is rice. It is like our base nature, based on our upbringing, education, and respect for our traditions. If we get our main dish right, whatever else is added in can be taken care of. So, if we each get our understanding of DEI (our main dish) right, the rest will follow.

'There are many stories relating to a few grains of rice in Indian culture. For example, in India, people will often keep a few grains of rice on the side of their plate before eating, which is a gesture to represent that no one in the world should go hungry or die from hunger. This is globalized thinking. Ultimately, those grains will be fed to birds or pets, but symbolically, they mean much more.

'It's also believed that even if you give just a few grains of rice to a beggar, you will go to heaven when you die. It's also said that giving rice to someone when you are also hungry is the highest form of charity because you're sharing the best you have with others. It's believed this takes you closer to God than worshipping God themself. There is even a tradition in southern India where you eat your first few grains of rice in the name of your God/Deity, chanting a *mantra:* "Thank you for the meal. Oh God, please provide a source or opportunity for everyone to eat so no one should die of hunger." As you can see, there is great meaning in just a few grains of rice.'

Thank you Girish, for your wonderful stories about tiny rice grains and how this relates to you on the topic of diversity, equity, and inclusion.

Prologue

Never in my wildest imagination would I have chosen to be the head of DEI at a multinational organization. Yet, this is where I found myself. Looking back, I have come to realize that my upbringing set me on this course, even though none of us could have known it at the time.

Sowing the Seeds for My Future

I am a third generation ethnic Chinese, born and raised in Singapore. As with many ethnic Chinese Singaporeans in my generation, my grandparents were migrants from China who had come to Singapore to seek a different and better future. As a child, I remember the many afternoons when my mother would tell me stories of my grandparents and how they made their fortunes in Singapore. It was inspiring and fuelled my young mind about the impact of storytelling.

My grandfather came from a relatively well-to-do family in China. However, due to the drought in China, he decided to seek new fortunes and opportunities. Coming to Singapore meant making some sacrifices—it levelled the playing field somewhat and he had to start from scratch.

But my grandfather was a hardworking man, with a vision for what he wanted in life. Back in the 1930s, he chose to work in the Mental Hospital (as it was then called) as a nursing aide. In that era, because it was a huge stigma, there was a shortage of staff and my grandfather was able to earn decent wages. When coupled with his enterprising spirit and determination, he was able to acquire land for a farm, buy a shophouse in the city, and also a couple of detached homes for rental income, after World War II. So, it was on that piece of land, on the farm, where I grew up twenty-plus years later.

By the time my parents owned the land, it had become a large commercial poultry farm in Singapore. We had farmhands working on it, and I would see them come every day as a child. From quite a young age, around seven or eight, I noticed that some of the farmhands never really talked much and were in the habit of hiding from others when the work was done. I also noticed that at least two of them would avoid eye contact and conversation, unless it was with my mother or when they were specifically asked for.

I remember asking my mother why they didn't talk or interact with the others. 'They're just shy,' she'd reply. I accepted her explanation, but I became aware that many of the farmhands my parents hired were 'different'. Although I don't know for certain, looking back, I believe some of the behaviours

I observed indicate that at least two of them could have been on the autism spectrum.

With no agenda or defined strategy that I'm aware of, my parents helped the underprivileged and marginalized. They did this by not only providing jobs, but by taking care of everyone who worked for them.

I noticed that my parents always took care of not only the farmhands, but also their families. They were generous with their money when one of them was sick and needed to see a doctor. Whenever my mum went to get groceries from the wet-market[1], she would return with extra food that she'd hand out to those working for us. She used to tell us that the jobs we provided at the farm made a difference to the people who worked for us and to their families. She understood what having those jobs meant for them.

Choon Kui, one of the farmhands who worked for us, was particularly memorable to me. He stayed with us for many years. Every day, he would show up for work and do exactly what he was hired to do. I remember being very impressed by his timeliness and work ethic. He never missed a day in all the years he worked on our farm, but I never knew anything about *him*. In all the years he worked for us, he barely said a word.

My mum spent a lot of time teaching me and my siblings about what it means to help others. She taught us the

[1] A market selling fresh meat, fish, and produce.

importance of giving people a leg up and helping them to grasp opportunities that they might otherwise miss. She had grown up in a very poor family, and wanted to help others improve their lives. She also made sure that my siblings and I understood that being privileged meant we could give something back to others.

I lived on that farm until I was sixteen, and I learned a lot about what it means to be kind from my parents. I doubt they knew about what we now call 'inclusive hiring' or diversity and inclusion, but they were exceptional in how they supported others. They simply did what they felt was right, without having the language to talk about it in the way we do now.

My mum never expected anything in return for her kindness. She was simply doing the right thing. She knew that if she gave back where she could, she would have a positive impact on others. A few years later, one of our ex-farmhands, Ah Teck, returned to visit my mum to thank her for her kindness to his family, and to apologize for stealing eggs to bring home to contribute to his family. My mum was moved beyond words that Ah Teck would choose to return and show his gratitude, and to be vulnerable about what he had done wrong. That was an early lesson for me in psychological safety. [2]

---

[2] Coined by Harvard Business School professor Amy Edmondson, the concept of psychological safety is the belief that one will not be punished or humiliated for speaking up with ideas, questions, concerns, or mistakes. It is the absence of interpersonal fear.

One of the most valuable lessons I learned from my parents was that doing the right thing was more important than being right. It's a lesson that has served me well in my working life, but it's particularly important to remember in my work in DEI.

The Best-Laid Plans

So, how did I go from growing up on a poultry farm to becoming the chief of diversity, equity, and inclusion?

Growing up, I aspired to be a lawyer. I had dreams of fighting injustice, righting wrongs, and helping others in need. I don't know what made me decide that I would be a good lawyer or that my temperament would be suited for it. I guess the options presented to me—accountant, teacher, doctor, engineer, lawyer—left little room for choice as maths and science were not my strength. And between being a teacher and a lawyer, the latter seemed to fit my 'rebel' and 'saving the world' aspirations better. Back then, nobody told me that there could be a third possibility—in diversity, equity, and inclusion.

So, with the determination of a ten-year-old, I had my future plotted.

When the time came, I chose to go to university in Singapore, still intending to study law. Coincidentally, the year I started my studies was the first year the National University of Singapore (NUS) offered a course in Psychology, and I was curious. Without too much thought, I applied for the Psychology degree instead of Law.

Studying the subject opened up my world. Clinical psychology was my initial focus, but I was also interested in cognitive psychology and wanted to learn more about the mind and how it affected our behaviour.

I pursued my interest in psychology by going to graduate school at New York University (NYU). After completing my master's degree at NYU, I returned to Singapore to work as a counsellor in a mental health setting. However, I quickly found that it wasn't the right environment for me. I struggled to separate my empathy for the issues from my sympathy for the individual and felt I wasn't ready to work in this field.

This was my first moment of truth.

After a very short stint, I left counselling. I worked for two years for the Singapore government, and then two years at the Michigan municipal government, before I took a job in consulting. I started at one firm, and then moved onto another.

A Shock to the System

In the first month of my second consulting job, I found out I was pregnant with my first child. I was surprised and worried, as I didn't know how to tell my line manager about it. I wasn't sure how they would react, or how they'd view me. All I knew was I couldn't avoid the conversation for long, so I found the courage to share the news.

I remember feeling nervous when I sat down for that conversation, but by the time we had finished, I felt I'd made the right decision. My line manager received the news well and congratulated me. I was relieved and glad that I had found the courage to be honest.

However, a few days later, I overheard my line manager having a conversation with a senior consultant. The senior consultant, who was a woman, said, 'See, I told you that if you hire a woman they'll just get married, and then they're going to get pregnant.'

I stopped in my tracks. I couldn't believe what I'd just heard. I was feeling vulnerable in a new job, was unsure whether I'd be accepted and was worried about what would happen when I had to go on my maternity leave. Overhearing that conversation was a shock. It was the first time I thought it hadn't felt right. I hadn't hidden my pregnancy from them—I'd told them as soon as I found out. But instead of being supported, I felt marginalized.

This continued with some of the clients I worked with. I remember one client complaining about me because they felt I didn't look professional in my maternity clothes. I was moved off that account and given other work. Whenever I tell that story now, the response is disbelief, but this wasn't uncommon around thirty years ago. Although I was completely shocked, I accepted it.

These microaggressions were wrapped up in a cloak of business reasons, but they were as unacceptable then as they are now. There was no single moment that made me consciously decide to pursue a career in DEI, but these little moments all added up.

My early experiences reinforced my view that I didn't want others to have similar experiences, and I knew that change starts within yourself. I made a promise to myself that I would never put someone in the position I found myself in, whether as an unsupportive line manager or an unreasonable client.

This was built on the foundations my parents had laid and reinforced my resolve to be a good human being. I knew that I would fail sometimes, but that I would always be humble enough to ask for feedback, and seek to improve and do better, if I did say or do the wrong thing.

I believe these three things, which have become my mantras, are essential for leaders in any area: Be human. Be humble. Always seek to improve.

When I was asked to take on the chief DEI officer job at Shell, I started to consider how I could use the privilege of my role to make a difference and create a positive impact on others. It made me think about my purpose in life, the behaviours I wanted to role model, and the legacy I wanted to leave behind. My hope is that this book will also form part of my legacy.

Introduction

Despite being part of the conversation in modern business, many of us struggle to articulate the tangible value of diversity, equity, and inclusion (DEI), and how it makes a difference to performance. Many also find it hard to see value in DEI or understand how to apply it at workplaces.

What I've come to realize is that often something that seems simple to us can have a big impact on others, especially when we come from a place of authenticity.

Using My Voice for Others

Over the course of my career, I've been a strong advocate and voice for those with mental ill health and disabilities. This comes not only from my upbringing, but also from my own experiences of mental ill health.

In 2009, I was diagnosed with hypomania, a mood disorder. The symptoms can vary from person to person, but in my case, I have an abnormally high level of energy, and I'm constantly multitasking. It had an impact on my moods too. To anyone external, I might come across as energetic and productive, but I have to be careful, because I can end up doing too much, which means I burn out. My mental health challenge is also cyclical, which means that I have to be self-aware, and manage my highs and lows as part of my life.

When I first told the company about my diagnosis, as well as some of the other challenges I was facing in my life at the time, I was met with nothing but support. That was when I realized I was in the right place for me.

In 2018, I decided to talk openly about my lived experience of mental ill health. I felt vulnerable when I went public with my experiences, but I also knew that I had to open myself up to talking about a topic that comes with a stigma attached, because in doing so I could give a voice to others who would otherwise stay silent.

It felt like the right thing to do. I knew that in my position, I could be a voice for those who don't have a voice. Going public about my own mental health challenges strengthened my resolve to continue on this path and cemented what is important to me.

The first time I spoke openly about this was at a youth film festival. I was nervous as I stepped out on stage. The auditorium was full. I looked out over the sea of faces that I could barely discern through the stage lighting and smiled.

The first thing I said was, 'Do I look crazy to you?' There was a wave of laughter as the audience responded with a 'no'.

Then, I asked them, 'Am I successful?' to which they answered, 'Yes.' They knew who I was, the chief DEI officer at Shell. These two questions really resonated with the audience and started to get them thinking differently about me and their perception of me.

I wanted to show them that you can make it, even if you face challenges, and that mental ill health can affect any of us. There is often a sense among those with mental ill health that you can never recover: you can never get a job, you can never be successful, you have to accept your fate.

My message to them was that you can be well again. To get there, you first have to understand what condition you have and to seek help and support to get well. You can have a job. You can succeed. Your entire life does not have to be defined by the stigma of mental ill health.

After I left the stage, people from the audience came up to me to confide that they were struggling. Those conversations made it all feel real for me. I saw that the more I spoke out about my challenges, the more I gave other people the confidence to talk about their own challenges.

It's not that the things I talk about have never been a problem before, or that they weren't important before. But these subjects are buried. People don't feel comfortable talking about them. By being vulnerable and putting myself out there, I felt I was providing the opportunity to unearth these issues and bring what had been buried into the light.

This opened the floodgates. People resonated with what I was saying, so I continued talking about it. I discovered that using my voice to advocate for others was another way in which I could give back.

Your Voice Matters

Being a leader in any organization or industry, your voice matters. Your advocacy, point of view, and support matters. Your influence, regardless of how small you might think it is, matters too.

On the evening I first spoke about my own challenges, one woman searched five floors in the venue to find me. She caught up with me as I was waiting for a cab, confiding in me about what she was going through. Because she had never had the chance to tell anybody before, she was wondering what to do now. Even if that woman had been the only person in the audience who resonated with what I had said, it would have been enough.

But she wasn't. Dozens of people had already approached me that evening to tell me how much it meant to them to hear someone talking about mental ill health so openly, and to see that it doesn't have to be something that defines you or your path in life.

When we become leaders, we are put in an incredibly privileged position. We can help people live different lives, for the better, when we speak up. We should not doubt the

influence we can have. We need to remember that even the small actions we take can have a huge impact on someone else.

Small actions add up. Every tiny rice grain has a part to play in creating a nutritious meal. This is particularly true in the field of DEI, where small, consistent actions are often much more impactful than single grand gestures.

Mind the Gap

All too often in businesses, DEI is framed as a 'nice to have'. It's something that people in a business 'do' when they're not 'busy'. Many more still need to be convinced of the value of DEI, but if we are forced to start all our conversations in this space by having to convince others of DEI's validity, we'll never reach a space where we can talk about what matters.

When I am challenged to provide data to demonstrate the value of DEI, I do not hesitate to point out that this information is freely available. All they have to do is to search online for data that shows that diverse teams make businesses stronger, more innovative, and more profitable. Diverse teams have been shown to be high-performing teams time and time again.

What I've come to realize is that the gap we experience in DEI doesn't come from a lack of data. It comes from how we feel about the topic.

In the engagements I have had across different cultures and geographies, I am often told, 'We never used to have a problem with this until we started talking about being more diverse and more inclusive,' or, 'We all just used to come to work and get on with it; we never talked about such things because we respected each other.' When someone says this to me, my first question is always, 'So tell me what it was like before? Paint me a picture so that I can try to understand.'

More often than not, we uncover deep-rooted tolerance for discrimination and microaggression. Just as I tolerated being moved off a client account for not looking 'professional enough' while being pregnant, many people tolerated this kind of behaviour because they didn't want to rock the boat. They had no one they could turn to for support or because it didn't directly affect them.

Another common refrain, often in environments that are more culturally homogenous, is, 'We're human first and we should treat everyone like a human being.'

This sounds very magnanimous, but it's so generic that it means little. While having equitable access is the end point, when we dismiss the research and the intentions behind the positive impact of embracing diversity and the culture of inclusion, it denies the reality of the situation and shuts down the conversation.

Frequently, I am told, 'Bad behaviour doesn't happen here because we are nice people.' I've seen surprised faces when I respond that inclusion is not binary. It doesn't mean that if somebody feels or perceives exclusion, that it is always

a result of bad behaviour. Similarly, being nice doesn't equate to being inclusive. Of course, it's good to be nice, but that alone will not inspire change and empower action to create a culture of inclusivity.

It is important to start with good intent. However, without practising the right habits and skills, intention alone is not enough. You might intend to land a plane, but if you aren't aware of your location and you haven't trained as a pilot, you have a high chance of crashing no matter how good your intentions are.

In my opinion, these views and mindsets are some of the biggest barriers to making progress with DEI. We all tend to lay the blame and problem at the feet of others. I understand that some of us may feel as though we do not have the 'experience' to talk about DEI, and this is why I want to bring the conversation back to what it is to be human.

We all have lived experiences, good and bad. We don't need to have had the exact same experience as someone else to understand what they have been through. We have to think more about what this topic actually means on a human-to-human level. To truly affect lasting change, we all need to be prepared to reflect and do the inner work. It starts with us as individuals.

That means using data itself to force people to have conversations around DEI won't get us very far if we can't motivate others to reflect, connect to their own stories, and consider making changes for themselves.

Creating a Platform for Courageous Conversations

Throughout this book, I'll talk about topics that might make you feel uncomfortable. I urge you to lean into that discomfort. I expect that much of what I talk about in the coming chapters will be things you have thought about many times over. What I encourage you to do is unearth those inner thoughts and bring them into the light through courageous conversations.

I can't promise to have all the answers. In fact, I guarantee this book doesn't have all the answers. But what I can promise is that I will share stories and practical reflections to help you be honest and courageous in your dialogue. And to help you sit in discomfort, talk about the uncomfortable truths and lean into the unknown, but come out the other side better from having been curious.

We all have to be prepared to introspect and answer these questions: 'What do I want to know but am afraid or embarrassed to ask?', 'What are my assumptions and biases in relation to the topic of DEI?' And, most importantly, 'Do I care about this?'

We can't shy away from confronting these issues just because they make us feel uncomfortable.

To encourage all of us not to hide from these issues, I believe we need to make the conversation more empathetic and more courageous, anchored strongly in our values and how we want to show up. This has been a large part of my work with leaders and teams in recent years: where DEI is concerned, my belief is that we start from the heart, connecting to our personal values and who we are, and this informs our mind on the actions we choose to take and how we choose to show up.

It's important to remember that our individual actions do not have to impact the whole world. However, that does not mean that our actions are not significant. If each of us took action that positively impacted a few people around us, it would make a world of difference. Rather than worrying about what resources or skills you don't have, instead look at what you *do have.*

Ask yourself: *What do I have and how can I create a positive impact with what I have?*

Chapter 1

DEI Conversations Are Failing

It's just before New Year's Day, and I'm at a dinner party in Singapore hosted by a friend from work. As we wait to take our seats for dinner, I chat with a few people, including a gentleman, who I learn is an executive coach. I catch up with a few other friends, enjoying the atmosphere, as we make our way to the table for dinner.

Upon sitting, the gentleman I'd been talking to earlier, appears to my left and takes a seat. Without much preamble, he turns to me and says, 'So, I'm not very familiar with DEI. Tell me, is diversity good? Isn't there a lot of backlash from the type of work you're doing?'

I am taken aback by his loaded question, and it must have shown on my face. Before I have a chance to respond, he adds, 'Why is there all this backlash if DEI is so good for business?'

My first instinct is to become defensive, but I know that this rarely leads to productive conversations. I take a deep breath, and ask, 'Oh? Tell me more: What do you mean when you say backlash?' At this point, he launches into a story about someone he knows who wasn't selected for a position because, in his words, 'a woman got the job'.

I can feel my face turn hot as he says this. I reply, 'I think it's really interesting that his conclusion was that the woman was incompetent, and not simply better for the position than him. Think about the other women who also didn't get the job, because they weren't as qualified as the woman who did.'

I could feel him getting defensive. 'It's not about whether you wear a skirt or not; it's because too much diversity is not good for the business. Research shows that too much diversity is distracting,' he replies.

By now, I'm thinking about sitting elsewhere, because I don't want to have this conversation over dinner. Despite my best efforts, I'm already judging him as a privileged male chauvinist. I know I'm not being the composed and objective person I like to be during these conversations, where I try to understand where the other person is coming from. Right now, I'm doing my best to not tell him that people like him are the reason why we need representation targets in the first place.

Instead, I tell him that there's plenty of research that shows diversity leads to high-performing teams, and I even cite a specific McKinsey report that precisely demonstrates this. We continue to go back and forth, until I say, 'Diversity isn't just about women. It's not good for performance if you have a

White man going to China and telling all the Chinese people how to do their jobs either.' As I'm saying it, my inner voice mutters, *Wow, that was passive aggressive!*

Despite our emotions bubbling just beneath the surface, we're conducting our conversation with a superficial veneer of civility. I'm pretty sure that were we in another situation, where we were free to be ourselves more openly, this would have escalated into a heated debate quite quickly. However, to everyone else around the dinner table, it probably looked as though we were having a deep discussion.

It probably won't surprise you to learn that this conversation concluded with neither of us having changed our perspectives. The reason I shared this amusing example is simply because it's characteristic of how many conversations around DEI go.

Opening Up the Conversation

We all start from different places, with different points of view. These perspectives have been shaped by how and where we were born and raised, our early experiences as a child, our lived experiences throughout our lives, and our interactions with others. But there are two ways to approach a conversation about DEI. The first never results in a positive outcome. It's what I described at the dinner party: a conversation where neither person is willing to concede their position or challenge their perspectives.

The second way is to approach conversations around DEI with a lens of curiosity. Ask yourself why you hold certain views. Are you right or wrong? Above all, be interested to find out what other's perspectives are and what experiences they have had. We all have different world views; we can't escape that. To make sure we can have productive conversations around DEI, it would help if there were established standards and expectations on curiosity as a mindset, and respect as a value.

Too often, I see or hear people having conversations about DEI behind that veneer of civility, like I did at the dinner party. This gets us nowhere. However, being able to have genuine conversations that can lead to learnings and breakthroughs require that we set aside our differing views. It is about being curious and taking time to understand the topic of DEI from another person's perspective. It is about being open-minded, being willing to learn and correct course. It is about being human.

Thinking back on the dinner conversation, I would probably have been less guarded if the gentleman had started by asking, 'Could you tell me a bit more about what you do in DEI, because I know little about this topic?' That question demonstrates curiosity for what I do, without any judgement.

This works both ways.

I could have asked him, 'Why don't you tell me a bit more about executive coaching and sports therapy, because they seem very different. How do you marry the two in terms of the work you do?'

Asking these kinds of questions opens the conversation up, because both people are seeking common ground and demonstrating genuine curiosity, rather than delivering a judgement and missing the opportunity to learn from the other person.

Finding the Win-Win

In my experience, one of the biggest barriers to having these kinds of curious conversations about DEI is that it is a very emotive topic. Many other areas operate within very defined boundaries, and the conversations in those areas have strong guardrails to keep them on track.

Take an end of year sales meeting as an example, where you're primarily dealing with facts. Did you hit your targets? How much revenue have you brought in? What's the profit margin on those sales? Those questions can all be answered definitively with data, even if there is a more emotive element when someone is asked why they didn't hit a target. Expectations are clearly set out at the beginning of the year, and therefore, it's relatively easier to talk about them.

DEI, on the other hand, is nuanced. Let's take diverse representation as an example—be it gender, race, disability status, sexual orientation, nationality, or other forms of diversity representation prioritized by an organization. It will not surprise you how the conversation quickly goes back to *why* representation targets are necessary. 'Shouldn't the best person just get the job?' or 'Why should we be looking at representation and why is that more important than performance?' or 'Why are we talking about certain groups of people getting the job, even if they're not competent?'

Diversity and performance are not mutually exclusive. It does not mean that if we're looking at diversity, we have to forego performance. It's not a zero-sum game, where for someone to win, someone else has to lose.

However, this perception of diversity efforts as a zero-sum game elicits threat and concern, particularly by those who are part of the majority, who may have benefitted from the status quo. As *Harvard Business Review* research reveals, there are three types of psychological threats commonly identified in this case: status threat, merit threat, and moral threat.[1]

Status threat means that those who form part of the majority assume that, to make gains in representation, some of them have to lose. Merit threat, secondly, refers to concerns that diversity initiatives imply people's achievements are a result of them being part of the majority, rather than due to their individual skills, talent, or efforts. Finally, moral threat usually emerges when people in the majority feel that acknowledging their advantages as a result of an inequitable system will tarnish their moral image.

---

[1] Shuman, E. (2023) *To overcome resistance to DEI, understand what's driving it.* https://hbr.org/2023/03/to-overcome-resistance-to-dei-understand-whats-driving-it.

As the terminology suggests, these threats should not be minimized but rather acknowledged with the same curiosity we would use to understand the underlying fears and discomfort of those who form part of these majority groups.

The Crazy Maths of Diversity

One of the most challenging conversations to have in the DEI space is about setting diversity targets to improve the representation of a particular group. While setting clear and meaningful targets drives progress, for a target to have any chance of being successfully met, everyone needs to buy into it.

Often, objections circle back to the zero-sum mentality, with questions like, 'Who else are you sacrificing by focusing on that target group?'

A zero-sum mentality could also mean that without a clear purpose underpinned by the right values, mindsets, and behaviours, under-represented groups feel threatened by each other when it comes to how diversity representation targets are set.

Another challenging aspect is that while gender and race/ethnicity are visible physical traits, others such as sexual orientation or disability status are not always visible. This is also compounded by the fact that we can fall into more than one group. For instance, someone can be a woman and have a disability, or be a member of the LGBTQ+ community and be from an ethnic minority.

You can see then how diversity target setting without a clear purpose and defined outcomes could quickly become a check box exercise. The more diversity targets you set, the crazier the math becomes.

When we explore representation through this lens, it is easier to see where my dinner companion's perspective came from. Perhaps, that was what he meant when he said too much diversity was distracting and bad for business. In my experience, the more we are fixated on the 'science' of target setting, the less time and opportunity we have for building mindsets and behaviours that support an inclusive work culture.

I'm not saying that having diversity representation targets is about checking certain boxes, but only that for them to be successful, they have to be meaningful and clearly linked to how it contributes to the organization's strategic intent, values, and business objectives.

Focus on Outcomes, Not Just Targets

One approach that I've found successful in defining meaningful diversity representation in an organization is to start with the 'outcomes' questions:

'What outcome are you looking for, when you have a more diverse team?'

'What does success look and feel like, and how will it be experienced?'

'How would performance improve as a result of diversity?' So, what does success look like? To me, it is diverse and talented people choosing to work at your organization, because they identify with its values, and how you collectively show up in DEI in a way, which is positively seen and felt.

In early 2024, alongside Workplace Pride, Pride Circle, and Solidarity Foundation Bangalore, I represented my organization in hosting a conference, 'Demystifying LGBTQ+ workplace inclusion' in Bangalore, and was also a signatory to the 'Declaration of India: New Approach to LGBTQ+ Workplace Inclusion in India'. It was an honour for me and my colleagues in India to host this event, and I was encouraged to see so many people come together to discuss a critical topic: the one that's an enabler for change and one that's gathering real momentum in India.

However, what struck me most about being present at the conference was the passion and resilience of the many people who were really striving to make a difference in workplaces across India each and every day.

To bring it closer to home, what this means in India is providing job opportunities for those who are marginalized, as well as leaders being visible and lending their voices to de-stigmatize the perceptions attached to the LGBTQ+ community. An example is to role model or lead in recruiting more from gender diverse backgrounds and highlighting the importance of inclusion.

It is also about practical things, such as access to essential hygiene facilities for the transgender community, which have been provided by introducing inclusive washrooms with appropriate signages at Shell mobility sites. In this case, if we come back to the question I asked about 'outcomes', we can say that such purposeful business actions result in creating a safe and inclusive environment for employees, also creating a truly inclusive ecosystem.

Personally, the reason I chose to work in my organization is because I strongly identify with its values of honesty, integrity, and respect for people. I also identify with its safety culture, where the organization cares deeply about people and has a relentless focus on everyone getting home safely. Safety underpins how work is being approached and is strongly entrenched in the DNA of the workforce.

Initially, I took that to mean only our physical safety. But over the years, I've come to appreciate that it also encompasses psychological safety.

This is particularly important for creating an inclusive workplace where everyone feels safe to express what we're thinking or feeling, including intervening whenever we see any unsafe acts or non-inclusive behaviours.

The other thing I look at to assess if an organization creates a psychologically safe workplace, where people feel a strong sense of belonging, is how they respond to individuals in moments that matter.

Ashana Heera, a Shell colleague from Netherlands, shared with me the story of her journey with endometriosis, and how her experience has been a profound testament to the importance of psychological safety and belonging at work.

'For many years, I struggled with severe pain and debilitating symptoms, only to be misdiagnosed and misunderstood by the medical community. It took over a decade to finally receive a correct diagnosis of stage-4 endometriosis, a condition that had severely affected several organs in my abdomen. The only option for me was surgery.

'The uncertainty leading up to the surgery was overwhelming, especially during Covid-19 and the pressure on the health system; whereas the expectation was that I needed just one surgery, I had multiple life-threatening complications and eventually underwent six complex surgeries in two years. During these incredibly challenging times, Shell's support was unwavering. My leaders and colleagues not only understood the gravity of my condition, but also ensured I felt valued and included—even when I was unable to work.

'What stood out the most was Shell's commitment to my psychological well-being. They provided immediate access to psychological support through Shell Health, bypassing the long waiting times typical in the Netherlands. This support was crucial in helping me cope with the trauma and anxiety that accompanied my physical struggles. My colleagues' continuous encouragement and understanding fostered a sense of belonging that was vital for my recovery.

'Shell's response during my critical moments was not just about ensuring my physical safety but also about reinforcing that I was an integral part of the company. They consistently communicated that I had a place within Shell once I recovered, not if I recovered. This assurance maintained my hope and connection to the company, allowing me to focus on healing without the added stress of job insecurity.

'Shell's actions demonstrated that psychological safety goes beyond words; it is about creating an environment where every individual feels respected, valued, and supported, especially during the most critical times. This experience has not only highlighted the importance of psychological safety but also reinforced my dedication to fostering an inclusive and supportive workplace for all.'

In Ashana's case, the outcome the organization created was one of psychological safety for one of its valued employees. But what if the outcome an organization wants to achieve is to build a more diverse workforce? How can we help people outside our organization understand that we demonstrate this level of care for everyone who works for us, regardless of their background? The fact is that diversity breeds greater diversity. So, our challenge, particularly in the currently less diverse workforces, is to find a way to attract new talent from different demographics. The solution is to focus on the outcomes we want to achieve, as the next story shows.

The Rocky Road to Diverse Hiring Success

My former colleague Olga Kortbeek shared a wonderful story with me, which demonstrates what we can achieve when we look at outcomes, rather than just setting targets. When Olga started as the HR manager for Shell's business operations in Krakow, Poland in 2013, the business was undergoing a period of high growth, and as a result, there was a big drive to hire new staff. Among the business case for hiring new team members, Olga and her HR team were also pushing to attract more diverse talent to the organization.

She recollects that there were a number of obstacles littering their path in bringing more diverse candidates into the organization.

'Back then, the Polish government had set some targets around employing people with disabilities, but they weren't mandatory.[2] Instead, the government was offering some financial benefits to businesses that achieved them. The problem was that those benefits were not huge. Within the Polish business world, there

---

[2] As of 2024, the Disabled Persons Act in Poland sets an employment quota of 6 per cent for employers with more than twenty-five employees (as well as all government entities).

was very much a sense that it wasn't worth hiring more diverse talent, particularly those with disabilities, because the cost and time required to onboard and accommodate someone in this situation was perceived to outweigh the benefits. That meant there were a lot of unhelpful conversations happening.'

But Olga and her team were convinced that attracting more diverse candidates to apply for roles, and that hiring the right people into the business would pay off.

'I was convinced it was the right thing to do. I kept reflecting and thinking together with our recruitment manager and DEI focal point on the business value we could bring by hiring more diverse talent. While we had many nationalities represented, why wasn't it the case for people with disabilities? As an example, imagine, there was a great person out there looking for a job, who was born with a disability or had experienced a horrible accident that left them disabled. They're still a brilliant person and, surely, we should give the best people a chance. So, I knew that there would be benefits to opening up our hiring process.'

And Olga says she wasn't the only one.

'I was so proud of and grateful for the team I had working with me. I had all kinds of wonderful visions in my head for how this could look and how it could succeed, but without that team who were willing to put their best foot forward and go beyond what was required, none of what we achieved would have been possible.'

Olga and her team were very clear that their vision wasn't about hitting a hiring target—they wanted to reach a point where they were attracting a diverse pool of candidates for any given position. However, they faced a number of challenges.

'First of all, we needed to understand if we had enough talent we could reach. At that time, the recruitment market made a lack of diversity a self-fulfilling prophecy. People from diverse backgrounds, specifically with disabilities, wouldn't even bother looking at recruitment sites, because they knew they wouldn't be considered by a majority of the companies. We had to work out how we could reach those people, and where we could even start looking for such talent.

'We also had to think about how we would position ourselves. We wanted to move away from the idea that we were hiring for diversity purely to hit a target, so we needed to attract diverse candidates, without excluding anyone else.'

The team took a creative approach. They advertised on various recruitment boards, newspapers, and job sites, as well as paying for adverts in locations like bus stops. 'Our adverts said, "We're hiring" and they all included an image of a diverse group of people whose needs had been accommodated,' Olga explains. 'That way, we weren't directly saying that we wanted disabled people to apply to work with us, but we were showing them and others that we would accommodate people with different needs.'

All their efforts paid off and, as Olga puts it, 'A curious thing happened. We started getting really interesting candidates, which was amazing, but we also started getting people who were not really qualified and who were trying to play the "I'm disabled so you have to hire me" card. We had to balance finding the right calibre of talent and skills, with having diversity among the candidates.'

Olga and her recruitment team took a very deliberate approach to this challenge by educating everyone on a new screening process to make sure the right people got through. But that was only one of many hurdles they had to clear.

'The next hurdle, which was even bigger, was working with the hiring managers. Typically, they would get presented with a list of candidates and, together with the recruitment team, would select three or four to invite for the interview. But the hiring managers weren't used to screening, or even shortlisting, candidates with disabilities. We had to put a lot of effort into breaking down mental barriers and making sure that our hiring managers were at least giving people with disabilities a chance to get to an interview.'

Eventually, things began to shift, and Olga still remembers the first time a wheelchair user was hired at the business.

'Everyone was talking about it. Of course, our centre facilities team went into hyperdrive, because the devil was in the details. Yes, someone in a wheelchair could get through the gate, but then the revolving door into the building was too narrow. But there was another door they could use, so that was okay. But then the rail for the trays in the restaurant was too high for someone in a wheelchair to use comfortably. There were many practical little things that needed to be looked at.'

Despite the hurdles, Olga and her team were leading a shift in perspective. 'It's human nature, but this is particularly true in eastern European cultures, that word gets around. Whenever anyone has any kind of success, word of mouth means that more people hear about it. People started to realize that we were bringing together a diverse group of people with different talents and skills to meet the operational needs of the business, not just to meet some diversity targets and get a small financial benefit from the Polish government.'

All of this took time—a good couple of years—before Olga and her team started seeing traction. 'The first year was a lot like trying to ride a bicycle for the first time—you don't go in a straight line, and you fall a lot. We had one person with a disability who joined us but left within a few months. This was because, although on paper, we'd convinced the hiring manager, they just weren't in the right place to work with and accommodate someone with a disability. There were also some success stories, and these helped us start a positive snowball effect. But it wasn't easy, and it wasn't fast.

'What we achieved just goes to show what's possible when a team of passionate and committed individuals come together—all sorts of great things happen. The road to success was really hard at some points, but we made it because we had a strong team.'

That said, Olga admits it could be disheartening at times, because they would invest weeks or months getting a manager on board, only for them to move on and the team to have to start from scratch. 'There wasn't a sustained culture at that point in time yet. It was very much a local effort, approaching people one-by-one, painstakingly. But by educating people and showing them examples of our successes, we were able to change the mindset towards diversity and disability recruitment within the business.'

Olga left her role in Krakow in 2017, but she's taken what she learned from her experiences and is applying them in her current job as an employee experience manager, leading an enterprise-wide employee experience practice.

'Building on my prior experiences and the conversations I had across the corporate functions part of this role in 2021, I realized everyone was doing something on accessibility one way or another, but none of it was really coherent or aligned to a common purpose. So, I started asking people in different parts of the organization what experiences we wanted to improve in the next year and created a natural, cross-functional team to make it a priority for the business more broadly.'

Olga also found that focusing on the personal experiences that people with a disability might have in the workplace helped her and the team think more holistically about what was required to create an inclusive working environment.

'To create a better experience, we really needed to step in their shoes. What if I were a person with disabilities, joining a huge company? I would probably have no idea where to start and how to get the support I needed. Where would I go? Or what if I were a manager of someone who had support requirements, would I be able to clearly articulate what support was available for them, and inquire further using language that was not offensive or insensitive? How would I position it to the team? Would I want a cheat sheet of things to go through? What should I remember? Or if I were a functional expert, creating a digital product, what else should I think about to accommodate various accessibility requirements? Using those personas greatly helped us focus on the right outcomes when it came to the experiences we wanted to offer.'

What I love about Olga's approach is her curiosity. She's asking questions and seeking answers to help break down barriers.

She also highlights how important it is that we start to think about diversity in recruitment *before* we get anywhere near selection for a role. Businesses in any industry can benefit from thinking about where their talent comes from. Do you always use the same recruitment channels? Do you target graduates from the same schools? Where else could you look to attract different kinds of talent?

Olga's experiences also showcase the importance of working closely with hiring managers to support them in making performance-based hiring decisions while also hiring for diversity. It's a mistake to assume that everyone will know how to support and manage diverse talent, especially people with disabilities where accommodation may be required. So, we always have to ask ourselves about what support our hiring teams might need, or what education they might benefit from, to help ensure that once we attract more diverse talent, this diversity doesn't inadvertently get filtered out at the next step.

Of course, the selection process itself is also important, because all of us have biases. A way to mitigate selection bias is to ensure a diverse selection panel, as well as to set expectations regarding a diverse candidate slate throughout the selection process. All of these things are small nudges towards more inclusive hiring practices.

The key, as Olga explained, is to start thinking about diversity right at the start of the process. It is about focusing on the outcomes we want to see, rather than the targets themselves. We have to ask the difficult questions around *why* we want greater diversity. When we can have these conversations, it can help us better understand what diversity will look like in our business or team, and perhaps bring about a more meaningful kind of diversity representation.

Questions to Ask Yourself

If you are in a position to be involved in hiring for your business or into your team, I've found it's helpful to think about what your expectations are for a new hire. Some good questions to help with this are:

- What skills does this person need?
- What attributes would be good for this person to have?
- How can this person contribute?
- What values does this person need to have to align with the team and business?
- Which diversity pools may provide the talent pipeline required?
- What are the biases the hiring manager might have and how could those be addressed?

Food for Thought

'To make a fish climb a tree'

In general, fish are not able to climb trees.

So, if a bird, a monkey, a penguin, an elephant, a seal, a fish, and a dog were lining up for selection where the task they are being given is to climb the tree behind them, then which of those animals would 'win'? I'm sure we can all agree that not being able to climb the tree doesn't mean the likes of the penguin, fish, seal, and elephant don't have abilities.

The Diversity of Disabilities and Enabling Accessibility and Inclusion

Olga's story has some incredible lessons for all of us, specifically around disability inclusion, and it's more important now than ever that we think about how to make our workplaces more accessible and inclusive to those with disabilities. It is likely that most of us will be impacted by disability in some form, either from an impairment, or knowing friends or family with a disability. Furthermore, a disability could be acquired by anyone at any point in their lives. With an ageing workforce and an increased focus on mental health, we can anticipate a higher proportion of employees living with a disability.

At the core of enabling accessibility is the belief that every single one of us, once empowered to thrive in a well-supported environment without barriers, can contribute significant value to our surroundings—at work and in our personal lives.

Although stereotypical views of disability emphasize wheelchair users and a few other 'classic' groups, such as people with visual and hearing impairments, the reality is that persons with disabilities are diverse and heterogeneous. Disability encompasses the child born with a congenital condition such as cerebral palsy, or the young soldier who loses his leg to a landmine, or the middle-aged woman with severe arthritis, or the older person with dementia, among many others. Health conditions can be invisible or visible; temporary or long-term; static, episodic, or degenerating; painful or inconsequential.

The UN Convention on the Rights of Persons with Disabilities (UNCRPD) defines persons with disabilities to 'include those who had long-term physical, mental, intellectual or sensory impairments which in interaction with various barriers may hinder their full and effective participation in society on an equal basis with others.'

In conversations related to what an inclusive workplace will feel like, I often ask those I interact with to describe their typical workday to me, and to tell me if they face any barriers or challenges related to accessibility. Through these engagements, I've come to appreciate that there is so much more that needs to be done in the area of disability inclusion and accessibility.

Stories range from a person who had to use the service lift at the back of the building to get to work every day because the standard lift was not accessible, to neurodiverse colleagues who find the open-plan office too loud and distressing, to an employee who could not attend an awards event because the venue had not been checked for accessibility and the slides/ illustration materials had not been designed keeping people with colour blindness in mind. These are only a few of the many examples of the barriers and challenges that our loved ones and colleagues face on a daily basis just to get work done.

Barriers to Access and Inclusion

The following are some of the most common barriers to access and inclusion that those with disabilities face. I've included some examples here, as well as some suggestions to help you consider how you can improve accessibility in your workplace.

Take a moment to think about your workplace and the possible barriers and challenges that exist. Do you personally face some of them? Are you aware of your colleagues or loved ones who face these challenges at work? Do you know how you can help to remove these barriers?

I appreciate that this can feel very overwhelming, especially when you first start exploring disability inclusion. When I started in my role this was how I felt: I remember looking at all the ways in which things *weren't* inclusive for those with disabilities and thinking, *I can't do this on my own, it's just impossible.* But, of course, I haven't had to do this on my own. Nor have I been able to do everything.

What I realized is that it's the entire ecosystem that needs to change, and that certainly can't happen quickly. So, I took baby steps. By making a commitment to focus on one thing at a time, I found it much less overwhelming and have been able to introduce changes that make a difference. Sometimes, it's easy to overlook small changes that can add a lot of value.

Table 1.1: *Barriers and Suggested Measures*

Type of barrier	Workplace examples	Suggested measures
Physical: A workplace campus (buildings, outdoor spaces) or associated locations that do not allow for safe access, usage, and egress by people with disabilities.	• No ramps • Narrow corridors and entryways • Poor colour contrast between elements in a building (e.g. edge of stairs, signage) • Heavy doors • High desks, kitchen and washroom facilities • Lack of accessible evacuation plans	• Widen corridors and entryways to enable wheelchair/mobility scooter access • Lower/flexible height work surfaces and facilities, providing space for a wheelchair to fit underneath • Accessible bathrooms • Choose accessible event locations • Use good colour contrast between building elements • Provide personal evacuation and egress plans
Attitudinal: A lack of knowledge and understanding, leading to stigma, stereotyping, and discrimination against those with disabilities. These influence and feed into other barriers to accessibility.	• Making assumptions about a person's capabilities and ability to add value because they have disability • Assuming you know best about someone abilities and/or accessibility needs • Pitying someone and making it seem that you are doing them a favour by hiring them or making adjustments for their disability	• Raise awareness of disability, accessibility, and inclusion (including stereotypes and their harm, strengths, and the business case) • Reflect on and examine your own beliefs, assumptions, and behaviour • Ask your colleagues/employees what they need to perform in their role or participate • Role model disability inclusion through your behaviours, making your workplace more accessible, inclusive, and safe • Visible and audible evacuation alarms

Information or Communication: Information shared that excludes people with disabilities as accessibility of those with sensory and learning disabilities have not been considered in design and development.	• Inaccessible PowerPoint slides that have not been reviewed and fixed using the Check Accessibility feature • Videos produced without captions • Virtual meetings conducted without captions • Not using alternative (Alt) text for digital images or charts • Using only technical language	• Set a minimum standard/guidance for accessible digital communications including things such as using Check Accessibility, contextual hyperlinks, using Alt text for images and charts, and captioning • Create guidance on accessible meetings, covering face-to-face and virtual meetings (e.g. captions, turn-taking, camera usage, and more) • Break speech down into smaller sentences, simpler language, and remove 'jargon'
Technological: Digital technology (platforms devices, services) is not accessible with and without assistance. Often related to communications and information, it can unintentionally create technological barriers.	• Only providing information in one format (such as online or as a hard copy) • Creating or sharing content that cannot be read by a screen reader/assistive technology • Requiring use of websites/platforms that are not accessible	• Share information in multiple formats (e.g. hard copy, digital) • Ask about the accessibility of any new products, software, or services you intend to introduce before committing • Use learning and development platforms that are accessible by screen reader

Organizational/ systemic: Policies, processes, and practices excluding those with disabilities and prevent their full participation or access.	• Only allowing for one kind of working environment and expecting everyone to work in the same way • Learning programmes that don't allow people to take breaks/work at their own pace • Policy that doesn't account for the needs of people with disabilities • Providing only one way to contact support service (e.g. customer service by phone)	• Enabling different kinds of working environments and different ways of working • Flexible working • Policies and services that include access for and support of employees with disabilities • Creating different contact routes for end-users (e.g. phone, email, and web form) • Learning opportunities with clear objectives and ability to stop and restart as required
Internal: Belief in the negative attitude, stigma, stereotypes, and prejudice about disabilities and the abilities of those with disabilities, by a person with a disability. Also known as internalized ableism.	• Consistently encountering attitude, stigma, stereotypes, and prejudice about disabilities and the abilities of those with disabilities. Examples: • Not using a support service because they are not 'disabled enough' • Hiding/not using necessary aids in public • Underestimating your own potential	• Raise awareness of disability, accessibility, and inclusion • Talk openly about the strengths of people with disabilities • Share the business case for disability diversity • Create personal/professional learning and development opportunities for employees with disabilities • Provide resources to support your leaders to support their employees

**Table summary by Cherrelle Williams, Global Accessibility Lead*

I remember one of my colleagues in the Philippines asking me why we didn't have captions on the global webcasts by senior leaders. Jason Romero's question set off a huge lightbulb in my head—why *didn't* we have captions on those webcasts? They wouldn't only help those who are hearing impaired but would also be good for anyone whose first language isn't English. The technology was available, and it created greater accessibility for almost everyone. I've found this is the beauty of addressing inclusion and accessibility concerns on many occasions, although you initially make changes to improve the accessibility of a specific one, you actually discover that these changes make the workplace better for everyone.

Be Part of the Change

One of the biggest myths I hear is that to succeed with building a diverse, equitable, and inclusive workplace, everyone needs to be passionate about it. Very frequently, it is assumed that the job of DEI lies with those with the job title, people like me (who presumably are and should be passionate about the work!). And the rest of the work is done by the other passionate group of people, the employee resource groups (ERGs). And for everyone else, it is business as usual. This may or may not surprise you: DEI cannot be sustained if it is solely reliant on (the) passionate people. Passion is great; however, it is more important that everyone understands that they have a part to play in building an inclusive workplace.

My suggestion is to make this part of your job, just like the example of my colleagues in India, who made the hiring of diverse gender backgrounds part of their jobs. Another suggestion to personalize this is to look at what your colleagues are experiencing every day. As with what I mentioned earlier about making our workplace accessible and disability inclusive, these are the opportunities to make an impact on individuals and also on performance.

In reality, what is perceived as 'apathy' or 'resistance' stems from the following fears: 'I don't know what to say,' 'I don't know what to do,' or, 'I don't know if it's appropriate for me to intervene.'

Despite the lack of confidence indicated by such fears, all the conversations I've had with leaders, staff members, and employee resource groups over the years, have convinced me that most people want to make a difference and be part of the change.

These conversations can be uncomfortable and difficult. We worry about saying something we shouldn't or offending someone. When we don't feel confident or competent, we end up feeling as though we're not in a position to do or say anything. This can even tip us into a fight, flight, or freeze mode—just like it had in the conversation I shared at the start of this chapter.

In fact, at the dinner party I went through all three of these modes. I froze when initially asked the question. I looked for an opportunity to flee, to sit elsewhere at the table. And I went on the defensive and 'fought' back against what was being said.

For most of us, when we enter fight, flight, or freeze mode, or even cycle through them, we fall into a spiral of inaction.

So, how do we counter those voices in our heads that prevent us from speaking up or taking action?

'I don't know what to do.'

In the moments in which you feel most vulnerable and incompetent, I would like to encourage you to pause and first understand why you feel the way you do. Initially when I started my role as the chief DEI officer, I, too, was fearful about doing the wrong things, especially when tasked with commenting on and making policies about issues that I was not entirely familiar with. I felt incompetent and uninformed on certain topics such as disability inclusion and the experience and struggles of my LGBTQ+ colleagues.

I started to ask for help to understand, I listened to my colleagues from the ERGs (employee resource groups) to increase my awareness, I developed my knowledge by reading reports and journals on these topics, and also tried to learn from what other organizations were doing. Most importantly, the first step for me was to admit that I did not know everything and that I could learn from others' experience and expertise. I slowly grew in confidence and realized that others were also learning by doing.

'I don't know what to say.'

If you lack confidence having conversations about DEI, perhaps because when you had such conversations before you accidentally said the wrong thing, my advice is to find someone with whom you're comfortable having this conversation and explore how you can build up your confidence to say the right thing. Practice having these conversations with a partner you trust. Bouncing ideas between the two of you will help you build your confidence. Along the way, I've learned that people want to be heard and respected. In fact, asking them about their experiences with the intention to make a difference empowers them and gives them a platform to share what they know.

'I don't know if it's appropriate for me to intervene.'

It may feel as though you're diving deep into emotions without any facts, but that isn't actually the case. When you feel like this, you can ask yourself two questions: First, what is it that I don't know about the situation? Second, what do I need to address? This makes your assessment of the situation more objective and provides the opportunity to intervene in a way that is not reactive or judgmental.

In every case, when you are feeling vulnerable or incompetent, take the opportunity to reflect on what I've shared in this chapter to provide a pathway to be part of the change.

Tiny Rice Grains Contemplation

Explore: What perspectives do those around you have about DEI, and what experiences have they had? How has that changed some of your own views? What have you held to be true and now hold a different and broader view?

Unpack: If you were to create a more diverse and inclusive workplace, what does success look and feel like, and how will it be experienced?

Your reflections:

Know (What do I now know?)

....

....

Feel (How do I feel about it?)

....

....

Do (What action can I take?)

....

....

Chapter 2

Why the Three Cs? Courage, Curiosity, and Care

In the past decade, research conducted by McKinsey through the *Diversity Matters* series of reports has provided strong evidence of leadership diversity improving company performance—I made a passing-by mention of the same in Chapter 1.

In its most recent report from 2023, it was found that companies in the first quartile in relation to gender diversity in leadership outperformed their counterparts in the fourth quartile by 39 per cent. Similarly, companies in the first quartile for ethnic diversity representation outperformed their counterparts in the fourth quartile by 39 per cent.[3]

In addition, the report highlighted a new finding—that leadership diversity is also associated with holistic growth

---

[3] Dixon-Fyle, S. et al. (2023) *Diversity Matters Even More: The Case for Holistic Impact* [Online]. Available at: https://www.mckinsey.com/featured-insights/diversity-and-inclusion/diversity-matters-even-more-the-case-for-holistic-impact

ambitions, greater social impact, and more satisfied workforces. The business case for diversity is clear.

There is much more research available to support how diversity benefits businesses across all industries and of all sizes.[4] I share this here only because the central premise introducing the three Cs of courage, curiosity and care are, firstly, that all data demonstrates diversity matters.

As part of its research in 2020, McKinsey had also carried out social listening to gather qualitative insights from employees around the world about inclusion and what it feels like to be part of a diverse team.[5] What they found was that in more diverse teams, people tended to feel more included. This meant people in diverse teams felt more able to speak up, and more valued. It was these social aspects of the report that really captured my interest.

It got me to dig deeper into why, despite all the research and data, we continue to spin the wheel on the business case for more diversity in the workplace. The noise around the diversity debate has become increasingly distracting and more controversial than ever before.

---

[4] World Economic Forum (2023). *Diversity, Equity and Inclusion Lighthouses 2024, Insight Report.* Available at: chrome-extension://efaidnbmnnnibpcajpcglclefindmkaj/https://www3.weforum.org/docs/WEF_Diversity_Equity_and_Inclusion_Lighthouses_2024.pdf

[5] Dixon-Fyle, S. et al. (2020) *Diversity wins: How Inclusion Matters* [Online]. Available at:. https://www.mckinsey.com/featured-insights/diversity-and-inclusion/diversity-wins-how-inclusion-matters.

My search to cut through this noise brought me back to my interest in psychology, and more specifically to social behaviour and neuroscience, which led me to the work of Matthew Lieberman, a leading social neuroscientist.

Dr Lieberman's research is grounded on the concept that our brains are wired to be social and to connect with others. It provides insight into how social relationships result in us feeling social rewards, which encompasses inclusion, being valued, and belonging. On the other hand, social exclusion leads to what is defined as 'social pain'.[6]

Dr Lieberman's research shows that when people are excluded their brain waves change. Social pain is every bit as real and uncomfortable as physical pain. In the context of work, social pain can have a negative impact on people's productivity and their physical and mental well-being.

I have also been inspired by Daniel Kahnemann's work on 'Thinking Fast and Slow', which, in essence, differentiates two modes of thought. System 1 is fast, instinctive, and emotional, and System 2 is slower, more deliberate, and more logical.[7] My friend Dr Kelvin Gee has an interesting perspective on System 1 and System 2, related to his background as a surgeon.

'When you train as a surgeon, one of the first techniques you learn is suturing. As with any skill, at the beginning it is very

---

[6] Lieberman, M.D. (2014) *Social: Why Our Brains are Wired to Connect.* Crown.

[7] Kahneman, D. (2011) *Thinking, fast and slow.* Penguin UK.

tedious. We don't know what to do, we have to try many times to get it right. Sometimes, we'll get confused, so we have to use System 2 thinking. We have to put a lot of effort into thinking about the angle at which we put the needle in, how deep we go, and making sure we suture at the right 'distance'. Then, we must learn to hand tie the thread. That's an interesting one, because you have to pay a lot of attention on where your hand is, how your fingers are, and how you lock the suture down tightly. This all requires System 2 thinking.

'However, over time, it becomes easier. Eventually you can suture quickly and accurately, without having to give much conscious thought to how you're moving the needle and where your hands are. It becomes intuitive. I would say it takes around two to three months for a trainee surgeon to feel like they are comfortable with suturing, but at that point they still have to put a lot of conscious thought into what they're doing. Although, if you look at a surgeon who has been operating for decades, I'm sure they could almost suture with their eyes closed because the technique has become second nature to them.'

What I find so interesting about this is that it shows how, with practice, we can tap into System 1 thinking with any skill. But when we want to learn something new, we will always need to start with System 2 thinking before we can act intuitively.

Without getting into too much more detail about Kahneman's book, what it provided me was the link and the appreciation that many times, our actions and behaviours that are related to inclusion or exclusion could be the result of the biases we bring with us—biases that are rooted in where we were born and raised, our early influences and experience, for instance. These are 'fast and instinctive and could be unconscious' and often rooted in System 1 thinking. So, we need to find a way to tap into System 2 thinking, where we can be more deliberate.

One way to bring about this kind of change is through 'positive disruption'. In this case, positive disruption means to introduce techniques to slow down our automatic response, to provide a different perspective, to introduce conscious action and choices.

I started to introduce a series of 'positive disruptions' in the way DEI was operationalized and engaged with in the organization. In 2020, I introduced 'Conscious Inclusion' as mandatory training into my organization as a practical form of systemic disruption. The intention was to bring about a conscious slowing down and overt awareness in the organization, and to introduce a deliberate pause for people to consider how they could consciously make choices that will lead to a more positive impact. It also creates more awareness of the negative impact one can have on co-workers when we consciously or unconsciously exclude. The negative consequences of social exclusion could be fight, flight, or freeze reactions. In the following chapters, I will share with you other 'positive disruptions' that I have implemented over the years.

So, how else can we positively disrupt biases and exclusion to create an inclusive workplace? This is where I'd like to introduce you to an approach—the three Cs—which has transformed the way I engage with DEI, and I hope that it can be helpful to you too.

What my team and I fondly call the three Cs is about having genuine and honest conversations around courage, curiosity, and care.

The three Cs start with the self, and how we can each contribute to create an environment where people feel cared for, seen, heard, and valued.

Get Comfortable With Being Uncomfortable

I started playing tennis not too long ago and have since been taking classes to improve my game. Recently, in one such class, I was practicing a new serve that my coach wanted me to try. It felt really uncomfortable and unnatural. When I told him about how it felt, he replied, 'Yes, and you'll find that after three or four tries; you'll slip back into your original form because that's what feels comfortable.'

When he said that, I paused our session and said, 'I have to write that down for my book!' My coach laughed. I don't think he realized quite how insightful his comment was. Our mental muscles that control our behaviour, behave in much the same way as our physical ones. They tend to return to what is comfortable, unless we consciously practise and form new habits. The three Cs approach is a way to consciously practise and engage our mental muscles, so we do not slip back into our old habits and biases. It's a way to bring us out of System 1 thinking and activate System 2 thinking.

Start With Care, Lean into Courage, and Show Curiosity

There are many ways in which care can be applied to create inclusion. These range from an organization's policies to how your leaders support you to care for yourself. Courage is about the action we take to demonstrate inclusion. Curiosity is making the choice to understand from another's perspective, and also the willingness to pick up new knowledge on an area with which we are unfamiliar.

When we are working to create inclusion, it is easy to slip back into our old patterns of behaviour, but remaining where it's comfortable and not shifting our mindsets or changing our behaviours isn't going to lead to the outcome of care that we're aiming for.

While policies and interventions at an organizational level can help, it is in how the policies are delivered, by leaders and colleagues who care about the impact, that change is really seen and felt. We have to be curious and positively disrupt our normal patterns of thinking and behaviour. We must have courage to take action that may feel uncomfortable but lead to the right outcomes and commit to doing the right thing when it's hard, not only when it's easy.

What It Means to Care

In general, showing care is easy if it is towards a loved one. However, what does it mean at work? How is care demonstrated? Does caring mean you give someone a listening ear when they need it the most? Or does it mean you make time to get to know a colleague better? Or do you think of care in a more systematic sense that you know that your organization will take care of you when you need it? In reality, it is all of those things, and more.

We all know what it feels like to be cared for, and to care for someone else. It is the feeling of connectedness, which is why the concept of care is one that we can all identify with. On an emotive level, we all get it, but the challenge is in knowing how best to apply that care in a practical way.

However, care is a broad term that can include everything from care for an individual, to the care initiatives at an organization-wide level. The simplest way I've found to apply care is to view it from the two lenses of care for the self and care for others.

We are all familiar with the 'inflight safety video', where we are told to put the oxygen masks on ourselves before attending to others, during an emergency. In the same way, knowing how you care for yourself physically, mentally, and psychologically is the first step to caring for others. What do you do to build better resilience? What do you do when you feel like you're not well? How do you ask for help if you need to?

Talking openly about one's mental health and well-being is not easy. It requires the willingness to be vulnerable, as well as the competence and confidence to support in the right way.

One of the biggest dilemmas leaders struggle with is drawing the line between caring versus caring too much in a professional setting. This is especially true when it comes to mental health and well-being. It is important to recognize that you're not an expert in the field of mental health and that the care shown is not about providing advice on what to do or how to get better. Instead, it is about signposting where the other person can get the right type of support and help.

As the topic of mental health and well-being becomes more mainstream in the workplace, organizations are investing in resources and support to ensure timely access to quality support and care for employees. So, how do organizations define and deliver care for their employees? And what is the appropriate type of care?

Organizations that have invested in building capability and resources typically address four levels of support, which create an inclusive ecosystem for employees to thrive.

1. *Self-help:* Tools and resources that equip individuals with the awareness and knowledge to adopt self-care behaviours.

2. *Supporting others:* Building competence and confidence to support others as mental health and well-being ambassadors and as allies.
3. *Professional (external) support:* This is typically in the form of an Employee Assistance Programme, where employees are provided with a safe space to disclose their challenges and seek professional help.
4. *Specialist (external) support:* This typically involves specialist support and care, including diagnosis and long-term treatment and management where required. This is usually included in the organization's policy and benefits on the type of specialist support to which employees are entitled.

The four levels of support apply equally to leaders as they do to staff members. When it comes to showing care for others, it is a leader who understands what support is available, how it is used, and are themselves utilizing the tools and resources available, which will create a safe space for their teams. It is the combination of leaders showing care in a way that is consistent because the organization has invested in tools and resources to visibly demonstrate care.

Simon Leow, co-founder of the Happiness Initiative, told me that a growing number of organizations are focusing on employee well-being and providing specific tools and resources to improve people's mental health, since the Covid-19 pandemic.

'Before Covid, it was difficult to get some organizations to subscribe to the importance of well-being skills. Many of them talked about mental ill health as though it only related to a minority of people. But the social isolation we all experienced during Covid-19 made the whole experience a lot more pronounced and more relatable.'

As a result, Simon has noticed more companies are prepared to invest in resources to help improve well-being, which he says covers three levels: the individual, team, and cultural.

'Some organizations engage us to run workshops or experiences at an individual level, and to help managers and supervisors develop skills to bring out the best in their teams. To see change at a cultural level, you need your senior leaders and board members to have a more enlightened view of well-being,' he explained.

For any well-being initiatives to succeed, we need three key ingredients: leadership and culture, that go hand in hand, while having the right people act as champions for well-being initiatives.

'The top leaders and the culture at an organization must support any well-being initiative. When this is in place, you will be able to select the right people to sponsor or champion your initiatives.'

Simon shared one particularly powerful story about when he'd seen this work in practice. 'One organization we worked with appointed a leader to be their well-being champion.

There was a theme for each month, and it was her job to tie everything for that theme together across the business. One month, she came to me and said she'd like to make grief and loss one of the monthly themes.

'We talked about the five stages of grief, and I shared with her that, in my experience, grief isn't linear: I could be in "acceptance" and then go back to "denial". It was all jumbled up, instead of orderly. She told me that her experience of grief had been similar, and I could see she instantly connected with the concept. We realized that we should talk openly about our own experiences with grief, because we knew we'd be able to curate a powerful experience for the other employees at her organization. But to make that work, we needed someone (in this case, her) who could act as a champion for that topic because they had an emotional connection to it.'

Being willing to be open and talk about potentially painful experiences is one way in which all of us can show care to others. In doing so, not only can we improve our own well-being, but we also help other people improve theirs.

When I think back about what my parents did to support the farmhands and their families, I am proud that they were role modelling care. They were ambassadors to their workers and created an ecosystem for each of them to bring their best selves to work. There is a lot of power in being able to see someone who's come before you role model for the next generation, particularly in the area of diversity, equity, and inclusion.

How Courage Leads to Care

> 'Courage' [noun] means strength of mind to carry on in spite of danger or difficulty. In Middle English, 'corage' means 'the heart as a source of feelings'.
>
> —Webster's dictionary

Vishal Kumar works at a multinational corporation. His eyesight started deteriorating when he was a child, disrupting his education, but he always had a lot of support and care from his family. 'I remember when I dropped out of school and hearing people talk about me to my parents. They'd say things like, "Your child is going to be dependent for life, what will he do?" Even though I was still young, I could understand that they thought I wouldn't be able to do anything.

'I took their words as a challenge to prove them wrong. My parents never told me that I wouldn't be able to do things because of my visual impairment. In fact, they never lowered their expectations of me and treated me much like any other child, but they cared enough to recognize that I would have to change my approach to certain parts of life.'

After a three-year gap in his education, Vishal restarted at school and eventually moved to Bangalore, where he learned computing, and completed an MBA with one of the top five business schools in India.

'When I started living independently after I moved to Bangalore, there were barriers, but I had no choice but to overcome them. You either look for a workaround, or you challenge those barriers and break through them. But you do reach a point, once you have the basics sorted, where you have to prioritize the barriers you challenge, because there can be so many of them. What I discovered by prioritizing where I focused my energy is that there are some occasions when I have to accept a barrier and that I can't do anything about it.

'But I also learned to simplify the challenges I was facing. For example, when I was applying for my MBA, many people said to me, "Why are you applying for one of the top ten institutions in the country? Why don't you lower your standards and be more realistic?" The programme I applied for, attracted over 300,000 applications for 3,000 places. But instead of worrying about the competition, I simplified the challenge: there were 3,000 seats and I needed one. I focused on what was in my control and on progressing towards that goal,' Vishal explained.

And he got one of those 3,000 seats.

What's remarkable is the way in which Vishal reframes any challenge as a choice—including those that many people would shy away from. 'During my onboarding, when I joined Tata Motors, the team was going mountaineering as part of a leadership and team building programme and the HR team asked if I wanted to go. "Of course I want to go," I said, although I had no clue how I would manage. But how could I say no without even trying?

'I went, and I fell twenty-five to thirty times per day, but if you're going to fall it's best to learn how to fall safely. I enjoyed it so much that I went back and did a mountaineering course. Then, I joined an expedition to Everest Base Camp, 18,000 feet above sea level. I made a choice to have that experience, because I wanted to stretch my senses. I'm always asking myself, "Can I do more with what I have?"'

Vishal's approach for himself radiates out like a positive ripple. The way in which he challenges and cares for himself allows him to also care for others.

'On an individual level, progressing from the perspective of improving your impact on diversity and inclusion is simply about looking at the work you do on a daily basis and asking yourself how you can keep it inclusive. For example, how can you create a document, or a website, or an email, that's inclusive for everyone? If we all keep doing what we're doing, but just factor in a more diverse pool of needs, it often works.

'Of course, you also need to step out and stretch your thinking sometimes. That's where we need courage to try new things. For example, if you're someone who's never hired a person with a disability before, obviously that can be scary initially, or you might have lots of uncertainties and questions. But that's when you have to make a choice—take the bet and experience it for yourself. The magic of what's memorable is in the experience, and you'll figure it out and learn a lot more by making the choice to try something different rather than not taking the risk,' he explained.

I love the way Vishal talked about how we can all be courageous in our everyday lives, and I'll share more insights from Vishal later in the book. By having the courage to make those choices, he is showing care for other people and supporting them in overcoming their own challenges.

Of course, courage presents in different ways, and we need different kinds of courage depending on the situation. In the context of DEI, there are three elements of courage that I would like to focus on: the courage to be vulnerable, the courage to intervene, and the courage to challenge the status quo. In the latter two cases, it's very common that we flee or freeze when we are put in an uncomfortable situation and feel like we don't know what to say or do.

It is much easier to find the courage to intervene or disrupt if we know we are supported, which is why it's so important that organizations focus on creating the outcome of care, and a sense of belonging.

Within any organization, there needs to be a clear understanding of the underlying values that everyone working there abides by. When we know that there is a common understanding on what is being valued, it makes it easier for us to find the courage to either intervene, or to reflect on what we've seen or heard that's made us uncomfortable and ask the question, 'What can I do differently?'

Leaders are expected to intervene in situations related to exclusion. They may not have experienced it first-hand, but they will be told about such situations and asked, 'What should I do about it?' or 'What can you do about it?'

An element of embracing personal vulnerability and adopting an attitude of positive intent to support others are the two areas that will help leaders navigate this discomfort of not always knowing when and how to intervene.

Bringing Constructive Curiosity Into the Equation

Curiosity is about having an open mind, a desire to listen—to seek to understand what you don't know and to take on new knowledge or information to help you learn or know better. It is about having a learner's mindset. This is a concept we'll revisit in more detail in Chapter 6.

What I personally find helpful in adopting an open mind is to be aware of my state of mind and be present so that I can recognize whether I have any judgement or bias around a situation. I find that I am usually more open and curious once I have time to check in with myself.

Just as Vishal so eloquently explained, we have to prioritize what we challenge and when. So, instead, I've found a good approach is to think about what you need to be curious about and to prioritize it, so that you can move towards the outcome of care.

For instance, it is not uncommon to see a wave of interest related to a particular under-represented group, especially as a result of an unfortunate event. All of a sudden, the spotlight is on individuals within this group with relentless curiosity to find out about their experiences. While this may be well intentioned in some cases, the outcome of asking people from a particular minority group to talk about their experiences over and over again leads you further away from care.

Coping with discrimination or any form of exclusion can create the burden of an 'emotional tax' in the workplace, defined as 'the heightened experience of being treated differently from peers due to race/ethnicity or gender [for example]'.[8] This has a negative impact on our health, leads to greater feelings of isolation and makes it more difficult to thrive in the workplace. Nearly 60 per cent of women and men of colour have experienced this emotional tax.[9]

This kind of approach, where particular under-represented groups are under the spotlight and scrutinized also leads to fatigue around DEI initiatives.

When we take away the noise around the DEI conversation, what it boils down to is how to create workplaces where

---

[8] Catalyst (2022) *Emotional tax and work teams: A view from 5 countries.* Available at: https://www.catalyst.org/insights/2022/emotional-tax-teams

[9] Bloomberg (2022) *Understanding the emotional tax on Black professionals in the workplace.* Available at: https://www.bloomberg.com/company/stories/understanding-the-emotional-tax-on-black-professionals-in-the-workplace/

everyone feels valued, has that sense of connection and belonging, and therefore where everyone feels included.

We want to foster a culture of constructive curiosity, where the desire to know, understand, and learn is driven from a strong sense of taking positive action towards an inclusive workplace.

Dustin Henry, my friend and colleague from the US, shares his reflection, which sums up the spirit of what we've discussed in this chapter.

'Entering into the bustling arrivals hall at the airport in Tunis, Tunisia, I was immediately overwhelmed by an amalgamation of unfamiliar sounds, scents, and languages. Amid the crowd of many local Tunisian men wearing the traditional Jebba and women being directed to a separate waiting area, I was struck with an awareness of my own difference. For as much as I could recollect, this was the first time in my adult and professional life that I was "the only". I was "the only" White male in the room among hundreds of men and women; I was consumed with a mixture of curiosity, discomfort, and awareness of the fact that I was different. Every glance, every gesture seemed to amplify my sense of otherness. I was a foreigner; I was but for an instant a minority in that arrivals hall. This brief experience in the arrivals hall would give way to an incredible three months working in Tunisia. I quickly became enveloped in the customs, culture, cuisine, and kindness of our colleagues. My time in Tunisia though is not the focus of this story.

'It was at this moment in the arrivals hall, where I awoke to the reality that so many of our community, so many of those who will read this, experience on a daily basis. While I am so proud of the progress we are making at my organization, it remains rare that I am the only White male in a room or in a meeting. I am acutely aware though that this is not a rare occurrence for my Black, Hispanic, Asian, female, LGBTQ+ colleagues, and those with a disability—who are often the only.

'When was the last time you took note of those who are in the room with you? When was the last time you were "the only" in the room?

'Is this your daily experience, is it the meeting you are in right now as you read this. Have you become so accustomed to, and normalized this feeling of otherness and difference that you have forgotten it is exactly this difference that makes you unique, full of value and worth?

'Or, if you are a White male like me, it may have taken almost two and a half decades for you to experience a scenario where you were the only, and on any given day, it is rare that you are the only in the room—what are you doing with this privilege? I often reflect on how I can intentionally pursue and create the conditions for those who may be the only in the room. How am I creating the environment where everyone's voice, value, and worth are amplified?'

The Impact of the Three Cs

Care is demonstrated by creating a culture where everyone feels seen, heard, and psychologically safe. It is an outcome that can be achieved through habit forming and applying the three Cs of courage, curiosity, and care to role model who you are and how you show up.

The impact can also be felt in areas such as the types of HR policies, and for whom and how they are designed and implemented across the organization.

A simple example is changing how parental leave or care-giving policies are framed such that they show care and support for families, regardless of family types, and whether they are birthing or non-birthing parents. The impact of inclusive policies far outweighs the risks of misuse and creates more loyal and engaged employees.

Having the courage to intervene and challenge when necessary will have a big impact on those around you, but so too, does having the courage to explore your own judgements and biases in different situations. Very often, within DEI, there is no black and white—only grey. So, having the courage to examine your own experiences and perceptions through the lens of your organization's shared values can lead to transformational leaps forward.

Change starts from within. We all have the power to change ourselves, and in doing so to have a positive impact on those around us—not only our colleagues, but also our friends and families.

What I'll share throughout the rest of this book are the practical steps that I've found helpful, that you can also take to harness courage and curiosity in a way that leads to developing more inclusive and productive workplaces as a result.

Tiny Rice Grains Contemplation

Explore: What else can I choose to be curious about? Why is this important to me?

Unpack: What can you do in your role to make your workplace more inclusive? How might that show care for those around you?

Your reflections:

Know

....

....

Feel

....

....

Do

....

....

Part 1

Courage

I've chosen to talk about courage and curiosity ahead of care, because I've learned it is these former two elements that allow us to reach a place where we can show care for one another meaningfully. As we shall explore shortly, there are three types of courage, and each builds on the one that comes before it. The courage to be vulnerable is a stepping stone to the courage to intervene, both of which lead us closer to the courage to change the status quo.

While I understand that finding courage for any of these things isn't always easy, I hope you'll understand from the coming chapters that there are small actions we can all undertake in our day-to-day lives to make some difference. One of the key questions to keep asking ourselves, in order to help all of us access a bit more courage is, 'What else can I do?'

As leaders, it's particularly important for us to find this courage, because others will look to us as role models. While that might feel uncomfortable, especially if you are still unsure about how to navigate conversations around DEI, I hope you will take comfort in knowing that none of us get this right all the time. Even when I took wrong turns in the past, I have learned from each and every one of them, and it has given me the courage to continue seeking ways to make a difference.

And I'm not the only one. In the upcoming chapters, you'll also hear about the experiences of some of my colleagues, past and present, about finding their courage in various situations for a positive impact.

Chapter 3

Courage to Be Vulnerable

Many years ago, and much earlier on in my career, I was relocated to work in North America. During this period, I was subject to bullying by a senior colleague about three months after I had started work. It went on for about eighteen months, but it was very much a situation where it was my word against his. I had tried to talk to him about his behaviour. 'I'm sorry you feel that way,' had simply been his response. He didn't take any responsibility for his behaviour, let alone attempt to change it.

The situation had reached the point where I felt as though my only other option was to resign. I felt I had no choice but to go to my line manager and tell them what I had been experiencing. When I told my boss about it, I was met by a stony expression. There was no reaction: no offer of help or support of any kind. I left that meeting feeling as though my work life would get worse, instead of better.

And I was right.

I felt judged every time I walked into the office. I didn't feel safe working in that environment. Soon after, I ended up leaving that job for one where I had a more supportive boss.

Fast forward to 2009 . . .

I knew I needed to talk to someone about what I had been going through, but I was scared. *What if they judged me? What if they didn't understand? Should I even tell anyone at work I was struggling, or should I leave my personal life at home and pretend everything was fine?*

These questions were going round and round in my head.

But I knew, deep down, that I needed to be honest. At the time, I didn't think of it as showing vulnerability; simply that being honest with myself and my business leader, Asada, felt like all that I could do. I couldn't see another way through what I had been facing, without being honest.

Asada Harinsuit was the vice president for the part of the business I worked for. We had a close working relationship: I felt I could trust him, didn't think he'd judge me, and believed would keep our conversation confidential. But this conversation wasn't going to be easy. I didn't know what to say, but I knew I had to say something.

So, I told Asada that I'd been diagnosed with hypomania, a mood disorder. I had been going through a really low period in my personal life too: my dad was diagnosed with Stage-4 cancer; I had decided to end my eighteen-year-old marriage from which I had two children—all this, while I was working a very busy job.

All of this spilled out as I talked, but in a much less concise, and much more clumsy way than I present it here. Somehow, despite the clumsiness of my phrasing, I had managed to convey that I needed time. All I saw in the person opposite me was a desire to help and to understand. 'What is it that you need?' was Asada's first question to me. I felt so accepted and heard at that moment.

'Let me know how I can help you,' he continued. 'And also let me know how the other people on the team can help you and we'll manage.'

There was no judgement in his tone or language. All I saw and felt was support. He was curious, in that he asked me to tell him what I needed, but he wasn't asking too many questions or forcing me to open up more than I already had. As we talked, it felt as though a weight had been lifted off my chest, and for the first time in months, I felt as though I could breathe again.

This wasn't a carefully crafted conversation. I hadn't gone into that meeting with a clear outcome in mind. All I knew was that I had to say something to someone, and it felt like the right thing to do. I had good reason to believe that Asada would be accepting and understanding, but as I've already shared, I had also been in situations in the past when my honesty had not worked in my favour.

On this occasion, however, I had correctly assessed the situation as well as my leader. The outcome of that conversation was that I was able to continue working productively, while feeling very supported. Although the circle of people at work who knew what I had been going through was small, it was enough that I no longer felt I had to hide myself when I was at work.

It wasn't until many years later that I found the courage to be vulnerable with many more people. This happened when I began speaking publicly about my mental health challenges. This courage came from a realization that I had reached a more senior position in the business, and that my story could help others. I saw that if I was able to be open and vulnerable about my struggles, other people who were perhaps experiencing something similar, might be able to open up too. I remembered all too well how isolating it felt not knowing who to speak to, or whether the problems I had been facing should be talked about at work.

But being open about this part of my life, on a wider scale, required a different kind of vulnerability from me. My concern became that I would now be labelled as *that issue*, and I would no longer be Lyn, but instead would be 'the person who spoke about their mental health challenges'.

As it turned out, I needn't have worried. My identity simply evolved—I became Lyn, a woman who is an advocate for mental health, someone who is open about her own experience with mental health challenges. I also lend my voice in Singapore, speaking publicly to the media and at public forums, all for the purpose of showing visible leadership and vulnerability on the personal, sensitive, and stigmatized topic of mental ill health and well-being. I realized that although I had some concerns about talking more widely about my personal struggles, they were far outweighed by the positive impact I could have on many other people.

By speaking out and finding my voice, I was doing the right thing.

Courage: A Trait of Inclusive Leadership

According to research conducted by Deloitte, there are six traits of inclusive leadership, one of which is courage.[10] Within this trait you find humility, which I think is particularly important. When you are vulnerable, you show the side of you that isn't perfect, and in doing so, you demonstrate humility.

Many leaders can feel as though they need to be role models of perfection. There can be pressure to come across as an expert, and to be mostly right and rarely wrong in your decisions—for leaders are often expected to lead the charge.

However, having the humility to be vulnerable with those you lead, to admit that you make mistakes, to accept your flaws, and to show that you're not perfect, leads to connection on

---

[10] Bourke J. (2016) *The six signature traits of inclusive leadership*. Available at: https://www2.deloitte.com/us/en/insights/topics/talent/six-signature-traits-of-inclusive-leadership.html.

a human level, which, as I've already explained, is crucial for creating inclusion.

This connection is created by exploring whether someone has the same values as you, but to do so, you need to know what someone's values are in the first place. I certainly found that sharing my story created more connection with other leaders. Many of them told me that it made them feel as though they could be a bit more open about sharing their own stories.

Our stories are all different. For some, it meant talking about their own lived experience, for others, it was speaking about their backgrounds, and for the rest, it was sharing their struggles. Sometimes, it wasn't about a personal struggle, but a story about observing someone close to them struggling.

The other thing that having the courage to be vulnerable creates is a safe space. By sharing my story, I discovered that I had built a space where people felt safe after I received many emails from my colleagues, and strangers from around the world, who had read about my story and just wanted to have a chat—including the woman I talked about in the Introduction, who had come and found me after my talk on stage to tell me about her own mental ill health.

Inclusive leaders are agents of change. They have the courage to reveal themselves in a personal way: by showing their imperfections, connecting with others emotively, and perhaps doing things differently than how they would have done in the past. They create opportunities for change to happen—both by having the courage to address challenges by being humble enough to accept feedback, as well as by being vulnerable enough to open themselves up to uncertainty.

When I spoke more openly about my challenges with mental ill health, I felt I had put myself in a position of personal risk, where I could have been judged or criticized. Having the courage to do this helped me build trust with more people, who recognized the risk I had taken.

Connection Creates Engagement

To develop that connection, it is important to note that you don't have to have been in the same situation as someone else or have had a similar experience. As a leader, the key is being human and authentic about what you choose to share, while allowing others to do the same with you.

For example, I remember attending a Pride conference in 2019 as a speaker. The host, who took the stage ahead of me, shared an organizational perspective around LGBTQ+ communities. I realized that if I spoke about what we were doing in my organization, my speech would be very similar to hers—for I didn't have a coming out story, or anything personal I could share in this space.

While listening to her presentation, I considered what I could add to the host's excellent introduction, which would be different, but still impactful. I decided to share my story.

I recall standing on stage, explaining why I wouldn't be talking from an organizational perspective. I also went on to say that I wasn't going to share someone else's coming out story, because that wouldn't have felt honest. Instead, I said I was going to share my story, which wasn't about the LGBTQ+ community but simply about my experience of feeling the need to hide part of myself at work.

As I talked, I felt quite overwhelmed because I could see the people in the audience soften. I could see people sit up straighter, almost leaning in, and engaging with what I was saying.

I created a connection with the members of that audience, by sharing something personal about myself. I lowered the barriers to connection by inviting them into a personal conversation, connecting it to the heart rather than the head.

Share from Your Heart

You not only have to be open to sharing, but your intentions around it must be aligned to your values. People will see that you're being genuine while sharing your story because you want to effect positive change. That will only come across if your values are aligned with your intentions for sharing more personal stories and experiences.

But before you put yourself out there in this way, it's important to appreciate what your own values are, and how they could align with others'. Ask yourself how your values are aligned to the people you're working with, or your organization as a whole. What is the common ground between you and the people you will be sharing with?

The next thing to consider is who you want to impact and why. Being vulnerable doesn't mean pouring your heart out at the first available opportunity. To have a positive impact, you need to consider what you can be vulnerable about, so that it has the intended outcomes.

Vulnerability isn't always about standing up on stage and talking to audiences of thousands. It also isn't about sharing your deepest secrets or biggest challenges. I might speak publicly about my experiences now, but that's not how I began.

My suggestion is to start small. Be vulnerable in a conversation with one person. Share something that you think will positively impact them. Lead the way in your one-to-one interactions with others as a starting point. This makes opening up feel much more manageable and genuine.

As I said, it took me many years before I spoke publicly about my struggles with my mental ill health. But it all started by being vulnerable with one other person, and watching the positive ripples spread from there.

When I first took the step to speak publicly about my challenges, many people reached out, including senior leaders in the organization, to tell me how brave they thought I was. I didn't feel brave. I had only done what I believed was the right thing at the right time. After I made the decision to go public, I progressively saw more and more leaders talking openly about their experiences.

One of the things I appreciated most was the number of people who approached me. They told me that although my experience was different from theirs, by sharing my story I had opened their eyes to the people around them. Other leaders started sharing their own compelling stories about their challenges, their successes and failures, and more about the human side of them, which others had not seen or realized. We are all unique, but it is also these unique and diverse voices that collectively bind us and make us more powerful together.

These stories are just as powerful when they're shared with conviction and in alignment with that person's values. If we are authentic and genuine in what we share with others, we create those strong connections, and are able to build our sphere of influence, while being able to reach and help more people. When you reframe being vulnerable and approach it from the perspective of who you can help by sharing your story or a small part of your life, it becomes easier to find the courage to speak up. The key is sharing something that means a lot to you.

The Power of Being Vulnerable

A CEO I worked with told me once that the reason he initially found it so difficult to talk about topics like race, ethnicity, and diversity was because he was afraid of saying the wrong things, and of the consequences this might have not only for himself, but also for the people he represented. However, I had worked with him for several years and knew that he was a strong advocate and champion for diversity, equity, and inclusion. For him, the vulnerability when speaking to a larger group was a risk initially. But in a one-on-one situation he was able to share more freely with me. This had a huge impact on me, because it made me feel as though I could do my work with his full backing and trust.

Now, even if you're in a senior position, it is okay to admit you don't have all the answers and to show that humility. Of course, this can be very difficult. However, if you find the courage to be vulnerable—like this CEO did with me—you will open up the floodgates of trust and goodwill with the people who are on the ground doing this work.

You can imagine the impact this must have had. My colleagues and I felt incredibly empowered to continue our work in diversity, equity, and inclusion and his words motivated many other people in the organization to pick up the baton and take this on too, because they acknowledged that there was still work to do.

Being More Vulnerable at Work

Being vulnerable is not easy—especially when you are in a leadership position and feel as though others are watching you closely and may criticize or judge you. It takes courage and also calls for humility to admit mistakes and personal limitations.

In working with leaders over the years, I have found the following characteristics to be present in those who demonstrate vulnerable leadership. I hope this will help you think about how you can build trust with those around you in a way that leads to positive change.

1. Prioritize your time and energy to address inclusion. This is about having the right intention behind your words and actions.
2. Put your personal judgement and biases aside to allow you to focus on what needs to be achieved. Think about what stories you can share that will lead to action.
3. Reflect on the values that are important to you and how being vulnerable will help reinforce those and put you in alignment with them.
4. Admit when you're wrong and own your mistakes. There is no shame in being wrong.

Being vulnerable is about how we connect with others, but also about how leaders show up for other people. We can't have the courage to intervene or the courage to change the status quo if we don't first have the courage to be vulnerable. Being vulnerable builds trust and connects people. It is a form of role modelling, and it creates a safe space for others to do the same.

Tiny Rice Grains Contemplation

Explore: What story can you share that might in turn help others?

Unpack: Reflect on your values. What can you be open and vulnerable about and how will this put you in alignment with your values?

Your reflections:

Know

....

....

Feel

....

....

Do

....

....

Chapter 4

Courage to Intervene

When we first hear the word 'intervention', we likely think of stepping into a situation to stop something happening, or to provide a warning of impending danger.

As with many topics in DEI, intervention is not always black and white. There won't be a right or wrong answer in every situation. Sometimes, it will be clear that you need to do something immediately, such as if you're witnessing someone else being sexually harassed or racially abused. However, in many situations intervention can feel like a grey area, and it can be difficult to know whether you should intervene, or how to intervene in the 'right' way.

The 'ground rule' for intervention is to make sure that you have a common set of expectations within your organization about what's right and what's wrong. Ideally, this set of expectations is also aligned to your personal values. Take a moment to reflect on when the last time you intervened in an area related to DEI was.

What was the situation?

Why did you intervene?

How did you intervene?

Two Wrongs Don't Make a Right

Almost twenty years ago, I was working in the US as a team leader and had a small virtual team reporting to me. There was one individual in particular, whom I had a challenge working with. Not too long after I left that job, in a telephone call with a colleague, I was told that the said person had left the organization. I broke into a smile, 'Oh thank goodness because that person was such a b****!'

I was talking from my context, and based on what I'd experienced, I felt justified with my comment—not that I thought that much about it at the time. After all, it was just a casual phone conversation.

As I hung up, my colleague Nadir, who sat behind me, spinned his chair around. 'Lyn, may I talk to you for a minute?' I agreed, and he went on to tell me that he thought what I'd said was wrong and inappropriate in the context of the workplace. 'Perhaps you shouldn't use such strong words,' he said. 'It makes me uncomfortable.'

My outward reaction to him was, 'Okay, fine,' but in my head I was thinking this: *You were eavesdropping on my entire conversation!*

If it made you uncomfortable, you could have just left the room at any time or even signalled to me. And anyway, you don't even know the context of why I said that. Maybe if you'd asked, I'd have told you the whole story, rather than you getting annoyed at me about half a phone conversation.

Even though I was wrong for calling that individual a 'b****', my colleague was also wrong in the way that he intervened.

The funny thing here?

We were both wrong!

There was no common ground between us in that conversation. It's very rare that I swear, so the fact that I used that word to describe someone should have been a clue that perhaps there was more to the situation than he knew.

But he didn't seek to understand or start a dialogue with me. My defences went up almost immediately, and even though I felt it was courageous of him to intervene, he did so without context. His intervention started and ended with him telling me I'd been wrong to speak about an ex-colleague in that way. For my part, there were a lot of emotions attached to what I'd said, and I felt he'd just jumped in without even trying to understand me or the situation.

When you intervene like this, you often make the other person in the interaction even more defensive and leave them cold. So, when we hear or see something and we want to intervene, it is always worth pausing and reflecting on how best to do that so that we can open up a dialogue with the other person. What can we do to make this a conversation, rather than a confrontation?

We always have to think of the outcome we want to achieve—often that outcome is to see the other person taking action to address what happened or moderate their behaviour in the future. In my experience, that is best achieved when there is time for reflection about how best to approach the conversation, rather than by jumping in to 'save the day'. When we do the latter, we often make situations worse rather than better.

Seeing Through the Shades of Grey

The hardest interventions to make are those where there is no clear-cut right and wrong—the shades of grey, where the likes of microaggressions or poor behaviour or comments that are perhaps on the edge of being acceptable get ignored, and, as a result, get reinforced. Many times, they are the most uncomfortable interventions to make, because it's not easy to know when the 'right' time to intervene is.

In the story I just shared about my colleague Nadir intervening after my phone conversation, this would have been a more productive conversation for both of us if he had waited, reflected, and then started a dialogue with me. Where there is no immediate danger or crisis, waiting and then approaching an intervention without judgement is a more courageous course of action, than jumping straight in.

* * *

Leadership is an action, not a position.

—Donald McGannon

My colleague Lara Magat recently shared her story with me. It highlights her experience where support from her line leader and peers was crucial in helping her recover from mental health challenges. It underscores the significance of consistent and supportive intervention, illustrating how being an ally can take various forms, even when it is not clear-cut, regardless of one's role or position in the workplace.

'I had several episodes and symptoms of bipolar disorder and generalized anxiety disorder (GAD), which went undiagnosed during my formative years. Even as I became an adult, I still didn't fully understand how severe they were. Until recently, mental health was not a topic that was discussed or understood well by most people.

'I was struggling to get out of bed, so I would come to work already exhausted. People would see me and think I was lazy; I understand why, but it got that bad that I started hiding.

'Eventually, I hit rock bottom and went on sick leave. When I came back, my colleagues started treating me differently. I felt like some of my ideas were easily dismissed, and I was being overlooked during some team discussions. It didn't take long before I went back on sick leave and felt hopeless.

'Shortly after this, a senior leader in my department reached out to me and asked, "How can I help you?" That meant so much to me! I didn't think someone even cared, but they cared enough to lean in. I told them briefly about what had happened to me, and they helped facilitate my return to work.

'Initially, I didn't tell anyone about my mental health challenges, but I was supported without judgment when I returned, working reduced hours. My new line manager and peers regarded me as equal in the team, which is what I needed—to be treated kindly but without discrimination. They did not make me feel like I was fragile or incapable. I was seen for my capabilities, not my disability.

'The team was also kind and genuinely caring, so I felt safe to open up about my mental health challenges. Everyone was very receptive and wanted to better understand what I had been going through. They would message me asking if I was okay or if there was anything they could do to help. They were also vocal in their appreciation of my work, which inspired me to do even better, and that was empowering.

'It feels daunting to support someone with a mental health condition, because it is not always clear how one should act or to support. However, it's one thing we need—*care*. My line manager and colleagues cared enough to ask questions when they didn't understand, to trust and believe only the good in me and to give me unconditional support.

'At the end of that year, I received the highest performance rating in my career, having successfully delivered three projects during this period. I couldn't believe it: the person, who once wondered if she would ever be able to function again, was now feeling proud of herself. It's been one of my greatest achievements thus far.'

It requires courage to decide to move forward and make an intervention, even when it is not a clear-cut situation. It requires awareness of your values and the outcome you are seeking. This will help to make sure you intervene in a way that achieves the right results and that you do so without the judgement of one party.

This takes practice. As leaders, sometimes we find ourselves in a situation where we have to intervene quickly. However, this doesn't mean we can't pause to consider how best to approach it. The clearer we are about our values and what we will and won't accept, the easier this becomes.

When we do this, we are also able to see the best course of action more clearly. In my position, people often come to me and tell me their stories about everything from micro inequities to stories of feeling like they don't belong. There are a range of micro behaviours that can lead to people feeling as though they have been suppressed, overlooked, or not welcomed by their line manager or their team over a prolonged period of time.

Microaggressions are particularly insidious. 'Go back home!' was the taunt that my ex-husband, a Korean-American, put up with many times when we lived in the US, even though he was raised there, and it is the place he knows as home.

As a young adult, I lived for a substantial period in New York City, Michigan, and Houston. There, I benefitted and grew personally from the diversity of people I became friends with. However, as an Asian living in America in the 1990s and early 2000s, I was part of the silent minority and the recipient of microaggressions, which were frequently passed off as harmless humour.

I've been called 'slanty' eyes and other derogatory racist terms, been told by an ex-colleague that 'Asian talent was overrated,' been referred to as 'exotic' as if I were some fruit, and have been shouted at, in the mistaken notion that I did not speak English and that somehow shouting at me would help me understand the language. Of course, I also had my share of being told to 'Go back home C*****!'

While I thankfully did not experience physical harassment, each encounter left me emotionally drained and distressed.

These experiences have taught me that what is deemed as harmless humour by someone else, can have a huge and negative impact on the person on the receiving end.

On the positive end of the spectrum, my experiences have also taught me that one can choose to be an ally, and to intervene when necessary, such as when a male colleague supported me in lodging a report at a hotel in London where I had been the recipient of both racist and sexist comments from another hotel guest and his friends.

In my position as chief DEI officer, my intervention is also to represent the voices behind these stories and to bring them into everyone's consciousness. I can highlight occurrences of exclusion and other unacceptable behaviour, and ask what we, as an organization, can do about them.

We have to be clear about the set of expectations and the yardstick by which we hold one another accountable. If you are ever in doubt, ask yourself: What would I do if I saw someone I cared about being treated in an inappropriate way? Would I intervene?

Often, when the situation is personalized, the reply is obvious: 'Yes, because that behaviour is not acceptable.' This simple reminder gives us a way to see through the shades of grey that mask small instances of inappropriate behaviour.

How to Respectfully and Effectively Intervene

About four years ago, in 2020, I was in a virtual meeting with a group of senior leaders and an external consultant. To provide context, this external consultant had a reputation for being controversial, and had a rather confrontational engagement style, and I always felt like he was pushing me more than others. When we were in meetings, he would frequently interrupt me and cut me off. He would do the same on emails, shutting me out of conversations.

It is my engagement style to assume good intentions and to give everyone the benefit of the doubt. My personal guiding principle is to give people three chances. The first time I observed this behaviour, I told myself that perhaps he was just having a bad day. The second time I thought, *Okay, maybe he's just not aware of his behaviour.* By the third time, when he was rude and aggressive towards me, I decided I was going to make sure he knew I wasn't happy. I'd also made my line manager aware of his behaviour and pointed out it was a continuing pattern.

The third time this external consultant was rude was in the meeting I mentioned earlier, with the other senior leaders. I was upset and went into a 'fight' mode, cutting him off just as he cut me off. It felt like we were having a battle and the whole time, I kept waiting for someone among the senior leaders, my colleagues, to step in and intervene.

No one did.

By the end of it, I felt exhausted and incredibly exposed. I'd been fighting a battle in front of everyone, and no one else around that table had seemed to notice. *Did they all think this was normal?* I thought as I logged off from the call.

As I sat at my computer, a message pinged up from Ron, one of my colleagues who had been in that meeting. 'Is everything alright? That felt a bit tense?' were the words on my screen.

I exhaled, *I'm not crazy, someone else did notice that.* But I replied, 'I need to talk.'

When he called me up, I asked him why he hadn't intervened. He apologized for not intervening and admitted that he wasn't sure if that was the normal style of conversation between the external consultant and me. I was honest with him about my disappointment that no one had intervened, but I also recognized his humility to admit he could have reacted differently.

I felt that someone should have stepped in, stopped the meeting, and given us time to pause and calm down. We have to notice the signs, such as when someone is constantly being interrupted, or when someone goes quiet and doesn't contribute, and take the courage to intervene. It could take the form of suggesting to pause the meeting and taking a break, so it gives time to check in on the person who we think is not okay, and to find out what's going on, without drawing everyone's attention to it in the meeting itself.

The way I saw it, Ron had sensed that something had not been okay during the meeting, otherwise he wouldn't have contacted me afterwards. In some ways I can understand the reluctance to intervene—there is a worry that you might do so when it's not needed. It can be a very uncomfortable conversation to have. Moreover, you're putting yourself in a vulnerable position as well. This is why it takes courage to intervene, because you have to fight that discomfort and desire to avoid risk.

The key to intervening is to think of the outcome you want to achieve. This really is at the heart of any intervention. In most cases, the outcome we are seeking is to diffuse the situation to prevent it from escalating. It provides time to act in the most appropriate way towards all parties involved. There is no room for any form of inappropriate behaviour in the workplace. Leaders, especially, have to take the lead and set an example for others to follow.

On reflection, what had happened in that meeting was likely that everyone was waiting for someone else to intervene—what's known as the bystander effect. This is when we watch a situation play out, hoping that someone else will step in and stop it. My invitation to you is to start paying attention to whether you behave like a bystander, or whether you take action. If you discover you're the former, what can you do to become an action taker?

A useful thing to remember is this, if you sense that something is wrong and you're hoping someone else will step in and stop it, then it's time for you to intervene. I'm sure all of us can look back on our lives and think of at least one occasion when we wished we had done so, but stayed silent in the hope that someone else would speak up.

I encourage you to take a moment now to think back on some of those situations. What were they? If you were put in the same situation again, what would you do now, knowing what you know today? How would you intervene?

Take courage from knowing that you don't have to intervene in all situations all the time, but when you do, you will start to feel more confident in the positive impact you're creating.

It can also be helpful to remember that if you should choose to intervene, you don't always have to do it in the moment. If you feel you need more information, then you can still take care of it later when you have had an opportunity to learn what you need to. An intervention could be checking in on someone after an incident, such as how Ron approached me after the meeting where I was visibly upset. By taking that action, you can then decide on the most appropriate next steps.

Checking in on the person who you want to support is always a good idea. It shows care. Ask how they feel and what they would like to do or have happen next. Sometimes, what you assume they want, may be very different from what they actually need.

How to Tell if People Feel Free to Speak Up in Your Organization

About ten years ago, Shell ran a campaign called 'Feel Free to Speak Your Mind' to establish a psychologically safe workplace and to encourage employees to speak up. It was also to create awareness of the company's global helpline, where employees could report confidentially on any form of inappropriate behaviour. I was then the HR vice president for business operations, and I was leading a part of the business that was hiring rapidly in a few locations around the world. Naturally, I wanted the campaign to target the new hires to the company.

One year later, we had seen the usage of the global helpline increase in business operations that I was leading. Should we be worried about this or was this a positive sign that people felt able to speak up and now had a channel for reporting that they had previously been unaware of? I felt that given the intention of the campaign was to create awareness about the global helpline, we should view this as a positive outcome. It also provided more aggregated insights on the themes of these global helpline reports and the proactive actions we could take as preventive measures.

Many organizations have a similar global helpline set up. It is a good place to look for data and insights on the types of complaints being raised and is a useful source of information on how and where more work needs to be done to address inappropriate behaviours related to DEI.

Additionally, other ways in which organizations and leaders assess if people feel free to speak their minds include employee surveys and pulse checks that gather feedback related to psychological safety, workplace inclusion, equal opportunities for development and progression, and the sense that there are enough channels and avenues for employees to seek support if required.

Becoming an Ally for Others

A study on allyship in 2021 revealed that those who have strong allies at their workplace are 65 per cent more likely to be happy at work than those who don't, 53 per cent less likely to consider leaving their workplace, and 86 per cent more likely to recommend it as a great organization to work for.[11]

So the question is: 'What can each of us do to become a stronger ally for those around us?'

Positive intervention allows you to become an ally for others, although this doesn't always mean that you have to directly get involved in situations that might be uncomfortable or difficult. A colleague of mine really opened my eyes to how to be an effective ally in the way he intervened in relation to daily challenges others faced. Kevin Smith, an associate general counsel, admitted that after he had realized the privileged and influential nature of his position, he pledged to be more inclusive at work, and be an ally.

---

[11] McFalls, E. (2023) *Latest from the lab: When the intent and impact of allyship don't align.* Available at: https://neuroleadership.com/your-brain-at-work/intent-impact-allyship-dont-align.

Among the many interventions Kevin made, one stood out for me because it was a small and simple act that came about after he noticed something wasn't right. He had noted the automatic doors to the bridge that connects our two office buildings were faulty. Realizing that they hadn't been working for a couple of weeks, he felt this might be an issue for anyone who had accessibility challenges. Not only did he lodge a complaint with the maintenance team, but also followed it up when the doors were not fixed immediately.

This is a great example of how to be an ally: It can be about being proactive and about making the work experience positive and inclusive for all. He intervened and took action to fix a potential problem when he saw it, without waiting for someone else to act on it or pass that responsibility off onto anyone else. He made the report, followed it up, and ensured the doors were fixed. He was true to his own values, as well as those of the company, and he did what needed to be done to make it right.

As he told me this story, I realized how many times in the past few weeks I'd walked down that corridor and over that bridge, and at no point had I noticed the faulty automatic doors. I could just press the button and walk through. Every time I think about this story, I can still see the smile on his face and his satisfaction at having been able to act and intervene to help others.

This is a good reminder that intervention is about taking the action that will create a different and positive outcome. So, if you see something that is potentially negative or that could be improved, the first thing to consider is what action you can take to improve it. There are many situations where we can take a small action and in doing so role model the behaviour of making small changes to make things better for everyone.

Taking small actions is also a great way to build your confidence and become more courageous in your interventions because the more you intervene, the more comfortable you will become with the process and the more you will see the impact of your actions.

Intervention doesn't have to always be big gestures. Often, it is the small, consistent steps that help us make the most forward progress.

Tiny Rice Grains Contemplation

Explore: Have you been in a situation where you wished you had intervened, but didn't at the time? What was it?

Unpack: Based on what you know now, if you were put in the same situation again, how would you intervene? What would you do differently?

Your reflections:

Know

....

....

Feel

....

....

Do

....

....

Chapter 5

Courage to Change the Status Quo

'This is a beacon of hope and possibilities . . .' were the words Michelle Yeoh said as she stood on stage in 2023 while clutching the famed golden statue.[12] She was accepting an Academy award for her role in *Everything Everywhere All at Once*, making her the first Asian actress to win a lead acting Academy award. Her speech was a rallying call to all of us who have faced inequality and discrimination in our lives. 'Never give up,' she said, and she's right. We can't give up on working to make the world a better, more inclusive place.

I have long admired Michelle Yeoh, who is not only a highly acclaimed actress and producer, but also an example of someone who has used her fame and influence to challenge the status quo and break the barriers of stereotypes. Yeoh's roles in action films like *Crouching Tiger, Hidden Dragon,* and *Supercop*

[12] Kelley, S. (2023) *Read Michelle Yeoh's full Academy Award acceptance speech.* Available at: https://www.latimes.com/entertainment-arts/awards/story/2023-03-12/michelle-yeoh-acceptance-speech-oscars-2023

challenged stereotypes about Asian women being submissive or passive, showcasing them as strong, independent, and capable.

Her journey from ballet dancer to action star to respected actress in both Asian and Western cinema has demonstrated that Asian actresses can achieve international recognition and acclaim, paving the way for more diverse representation in the industry and showing what's possible when you don't give up the fight.

Her achievements on screen are far from her only accolades and legacy. She has also been recognized for her contributions to the film industry, including being appointed as a UNDP Goodwill Ambassador in 2016, where she used her platform to advocate for gender equality and women's rights, amplifying the voices of women around the world and promoting positive change.

I consider Michelle Yeoh as one of my role models because she has inspired Asian women to pursue their passions and ambitions, encouraging empowerment and self-confidence. And as an advocate, she has shattered stereotypes, opened doors, and empowered countless individuals to embrace their identities and pursue their goals with confidence and determination. Even though we aren't all public figures or high-profile advocates like Michelle Yeoh, there are many others who are the same in terms of purpose, and are prepared to challenge the status quo, through actions big and small, in their work and day-to-day lives.

Taking the Lead . . . With a Tank

My former colleague Donny Ching, who retired as the chief legal officer at Shell in 2023, has long been an advocate for DEI. During his time at Shell, he helped move the agenda forward in many ways, but he was only able to do that because he found the courage to change the status quo.

'I was the first member of Shell's executive committee (EC) [the group that reports to the CEO] that did not come from London or The Hague. When I was appointed, there was an outpouring of support from all over the world. As expected, the Asian community were particularly proud, but a particular interaction took me completely by surprise.

'I was at a dinner, sat next to a colleague from Nigeria, who turned to me and said, "Nigeria is so proud of you." I was a little confused, as I have no direct connection to Nigeria, so I requested him to tell me more. What he said next was a real 'a-ha' moment for me.

'He looked me in the eyes and said, "Donny, you give all of us, who are a minority, hope." This was when I realized that many people saw me as someone who broke through, even though I didn't think I was anything special.

'It gave special meaning to the phrase "I cannot be what I cannot see".

This realization was what gave Donny the courage to speak up for inclusion and diversity at every available opportunity, but it wasn't easy, especially at the start.

'I was very aware that I was a symbol of what could be achieved and that people saw me as a beacon of hope, and I was worried that I would fail them if I didn't advocate more for them.

'I also remembered that earlier in my career, one of my senior leaders took me to one side and said, "Donny, it's great that you're so passionate about diversity, but as you get more senior you cannot just be the diversity guy." Those words stuck with me, and as I got more senior, I would sometimes find myself holding back because I didn't want to be the broken record that was always talking about diversity. But I came to realize that I needed to be "the diversity guy" because if I didn't push it, who else would? I had to champion diversity, because I was the only member of a minority group on the EC then.

'I wanted to show everyone that I was serious about diversity and that I wasn't going to go away, so I changed my logo on Microsoft Teams [a team collaboration application] to be a very visible rainbow-coloured Shell oil storage tank. I wanted something that would be powerful and effective, and that would resonate with parts of the business, like manufacturing. I also wanted it to stand out.'

Donny's visible allyship as a senior leader signalled opportunities for other visible signs of allyship such as wearing a rainbow-coloured lanyard, which became a common and universal sign of allyship across the organization globally.

'As you progress in an organization, your calendar becomes more crowded and your inbox gets even more full, so critical business issues are what come to the fore and DEI sometimes gets pushed down in the list of priorities. It's not that other senior leaders didn't care, but I knew I needed to be the voice in the room who kept pushing DEI further up the agenda,' Donny explained.

But that's not to say Donny only focused on diversity in his role. One of the insights he shared is that it's crucial to pick the right time to introduce something that might be seen as a challenge or a risk.

'I always did a lot of what I called "foundation building", where I'd have discussions with people outside of the meeting room and test the temperature of the people on the EC to make sure that when I brought a suggestion around DEI to a meeting, I knew we would be able to discuss it constructively. You have to leverage everybody and everything in the room to get the outcome you want.'

Stepping Into Our Power

As leaders, we have to recognize that the power of what we do and say is tremendous, and in many cases disproportionate. I am still surprised when people thank me for talking about a particular topic or drawing attention to certain issues. It is important to realize that even if what we're saying is uncomfortable and takes courage, we shouldn't underestimate the visibility and voice we can lend to issues that we speak out about.

For Donny, his desire to be an advocate for others and to speak out about unfairness started at a very early age.

'My older sister had polio at the age of five, and she's disabled as a result. She has to walk with callipers and crutches, and I remember growing up that she often faced challenges: She couldn't go to certain places. I even remember my parents discussing whether she should go to university or not, due to her disability. This was over thirty years ago, and universities were not very disability friendly, so even though my sister is incredibly capable and wonderful, my parents decided she shouldn't go. I remember thinking, "Why can't she go to university if my brother and I can?" For me, there was a strong sense of unjustness and unfairness. I think that played quite a big role in influencing who I am.

'I'm not particularly religious, but I remember thinking about my purpose on this earth and what my footprint would be, what impact I would leave behind. As a result, I think I'll always be championing causes. I'm sure it's part of why I became a lawyer, because I wanted to play my part in making the world a fairer place.'

When Donny joined Shell, he found there was a huge platform to learn and to influence. 'Shell has a tremendous voice, reputation, network, and resources. When I joined and discovered I had such a fantastic platform, it felt like an incredible opportunity. As I rose in seniority, my platform grew and even though that was great in many ways, I was also fearful that I wouldn't take advantage of all that was available to have the greatest possible impact. I find it ironic that a fear of failure can not only compel you to do things, but also prevent you from doing things because you are so scared of what will happen if you do fail. What pushed me to take action, rather than shy away from it, was the knowledge that so many people were relying on me to do so.'

As Donny noted, conversations and decisions around DEI can often get pushed down the agenda in favour of 'more urgent' matters. There is also no definitive right or wrong in many cases, and that can make it a challenge to navigate. This is when having the courage to be vulnerable is important.

'DEI is not about logic and common sense. Most people in this day and age understand the business logic for it. It's about emotions. It's about having those uncomfortable conversations and making people feel the need for change. But to tap into that emotional response we need to be vulnerable as leaders, and there are many ways to do that.

'The more senior you get, the more you are expected to know, but the irony is that the more senior you get, often the less you know about specific topics. I remember in one meeting we had a talk from some of our technology leads about AI and cybersecurity. When they finished, I told them that it was great that they had come to talk to us about it and get our views on the cybersecurity and AI strategy, but that actually we were some of the *least* qualified people to opine on this. "We're all dinosaurs when it comes to technology!" I remember saying, and I wasn't joking. None of us in that room were the most up to date in this area.

'Sometimes, as a leader, you have to admit when you don't know the answers, and you have to rely on others within the organization to come up with ideas. Our role is to encourage that flow of ideas so that we don't just maintain the status quo, but instead, are able to effect change, not just in DEI, but in any area of the business.'

Starting the Conversation

For these ideas and opportunities to come to light, we need to know they exist, and that means we have to be willing to talk about them. Starting these conversations at every level of an organization is crucial for delivering progress in DEI, as Vishal, who you heard from in Chapter 2, explained to me.

'In my work, I get to travel internationally and I observed a few things that were not really inclusive, or that could get better. So, I started a conversation with the leadership team about how to make the travel experience more inclusive, and then, I went on to get involved in a representative group of customers where we talked about what could get better. As a result of this, we've launched a pilot programme of a travel help desk that will take care of your accessibility and inclusion needs when you travel.

'Another approach I've taken is to have conversations with the teams directly involved in providing an experience that is not as accessible or inclusive as it could be. For example, I approached our learning operations team because I found a mandatory course that was not accessible. I knew they wouldn't be able to fix it in two days or even two months, but by raising the issue, I opened up the conversation about what we can do to fix it. If it's a mandatory course, it needs to be accessible, but if no one tells the learning operations team what could be improved, they won't know they need to fix it.'

Vishal takes a proactive and positive approach to problem solving, and in doing so, he changes the status quo by providing feedback in a way that results in positive action. He not only considers his own experiences as someone who is visually impaired, but also the experiences of others.

'Most of my inspiration comes from my own experiences, but sometimes, it will be an idea as a result of hearing my peers talk about something that could get better. And sometimes, we just have to look at things from a new perspective. For example, when most organizations look at improving DEI, they start with creating awareness and compliance. Over the last few years, I've realized we do those things well in my organization, so then I started looking at how we could move towards the next phase: creating an accessible infrastructure, be it in the physical or digital work environment.

'So, I set up a work group under one of the employee resource groups (ERGs) in Bangalore that focused on information and communication accessibility. Our primary question was, "How can we help IT professionals with embedding accessibility into the way in which work gets done?" Some of the things we've developed as a result are training programmes on how to create accessible documents and how to make your design inclusive.

'We've also taken a creative approach and organized all-inclusive sports events, such as a session where people could come and experience what it's like for a blind person to play chess, or for a wheelchair user to play basketball. That led to a broader conversation around inclusive design.'

What Vishal has beautifully demonstrated with these examples is how all of us, no matter our level of seniority, can work together to make our workplaces more inclusive. Taking time to reflect and ask, 'What could we do better?' is a great starting point for these conversations.

Shining the Spotlight on Inclusion in the Right Way

As Donny shared, often it is also important to be honest about what we *don't* know. In my first year in my role as head of DEI,

I was aware that one of the areas I wanted to learn more about was the LGBTQ+ community and what inclusion means in this area. I found it uncomfortable because I was well aware that the acceptance, divisiveness, and awareness of this topic is very dependent on which part of the world you are in, and for a multinational business, it presents its own challenges while navigating them.

But I wanted to be an ally for this community. I wanted to actively and visibly contribute to creating a culture of inclusion where my LGBTQ+ colleagues feel a sense of belonging and are able to bring their best selves to work. One thing I learned early on was that small gestures and encouragement matter. Even just making the time to get to know someone better and gain a new perspective can have a big impact. Often, what can feel like a small step for you as an ally, can have a big impact on the people you are being an ally to.

One great example is wearing a rainbow lanyard at work. By doing so, I am visible as an LGBTQ+ ally and giving support to my colleagues. It's a small action I can take to challenge the status quo.

But sometimes, we need to do more. During the lockdowns due to the Covid-19 pandemic in 2020, my eyes were opened to the specific challenges my LGBTQ+ colleagues had—as I'm sure they did to many others in the community around the world. The pressure was particularly acute for those who were not yet out and who were finding it challenging to reveal aspects of their private lives. I realized how I had taken it for granted that having virtual meetings with the cameras on for every meeting, every day of the week was a norm. However, for others, it may reveal personal aspects such as living arrangements, an individual's partner, and other areas that may have been kept private. It takes a lot of effort to hide parts of yourself and not bring your best self to work physically, much less when you are working remotely, from your home.

Imagine having to hide something daily. It depletes your energy, causes a distraction, and quickly takes a toll on your overall well-being. When you add in the sense of isolation many of us felt as a result of the lockdowns during the pandemic, it's easy to see how this could spiral into a potential mental health challenge.

My Employee Resource Group colleagues and I had been working to create an LGBTQ+ Global Forum. Coincidentally, it was ready to launch in April 2020, giving us a greater impetus to bring the Shell LGBTQ+ community together during this time of physical isolation.

We had four main aims with the forum:

1. Support: To build a safe (and virtual) zone for people to come out and feel supported.
2. Learn: To develop an LGBTQ+ centre of expertise to provide learning resources, guidance, best practice and

to act as a sounding board on policy matters affecting LGBTQ+ staff.

3. Act: To support internal and external activities which bring the LGBTQ+ community together.
4. Engage: To develop LGBTQ+ ambassadors who can also give back to the community.

Since this forum was created, there has been a visible shift in the types of conversations from, 'Why are we talking about this (LGBTQ+)?' to 'How can we support someone who is not out?'

Others have observed the ever-increasing levels of support for our LGBTQ+ community among members of the organization's senior leadership team. On a personal level, I have grown in confidence in this area, and this has reaffirmed that leading in this space is about learning, leaning in, and being willing to be vulnerable. Of course, there is so much more that can be done, and by drawing on the collective wisdom of the group, we can make great strides forward together.

I don't have all the answers, but I do know I want to continue having the courage to advocate for inclusion and work towards embedding LGBTQ+ workplace inclusion.

While it is a very human dilemma to explore how to move the needle on issues such as this, there is one question that I have found useful to return to, not just in relation to LGBTQ+ inclusion, but in relation to inclusivity as a whole: How can we affect lasting change in a way that brings everyone with us?

Creating Psychologically Safe Workplaces

Psychological safety is essential if we are to create more inclusive workplaces. By making everyone feel as though they are able to be their best selves at work and by giving people opportunities to voice their concerns or struggles in any area of their lives, we can affect lasting change and bring everyone with us. To do this, I've found it's best to focus on our human-ness first, and the area we are trying to change second.

I saw this in action back in 2019, when I was a speaker at the 9th International Conference for Together Against Stigma. Over 500 delegates from twenty-four countries attended that conference and discussed how to put an end to the stigmatization of people with mental health conditions.

In many parts of Asia, mental ill health is still seen as a personal matter and, therefore, not considered one to be discussed in the workplace. But we all know that mental ill health can be disabling for individuals, impacting their well-being as well as business and safety performance. The growing body of evidence in this field has helped to shift mindsets and has made the topic of mental health, mental illness, and mental well-being more easily discussed in the workplace. This can only be a good thing.

The key to opening up those conversations, ensuring we keep having them as much as is necessary, is creating psychological safety for those who work for us. Through my work and personal experiences in this area, I often suggest organizations that want to improve psychological safety focus on these steps:

- Focus on holistic well-being, where physical and mental health are both considered equally important.
- Have health policies that provide mental health assessments and support.
- Be a caring leader to help create a safe workplace where people can ask for help if they are struggling.
- Be a supportive colleague and show kindness if you notice someone is struggling. Sometimes just asking, 'Are you okay?' is all it takes.

Creating psychological safety in our workplaces takes time and effort from everyone who is part of an organization. There are no overnight solutions. All we can do as individuals is show up each day with the intention of supporting our colleagues however we can. And those of us with more influence in leadership positions, we can do as Donny suggested, and seek opportunities to keep discussions about DEI at the top of the agenda.

I've also learned that a sign of a psychologically safe workplace isn't necessarily that people are talking about things like mental ill health all the time, but that they feel comfortable enough to ask for help when they need it. If you're a manager, you'll know that you can't tell someone 'they need help'. Even if that person's performance is being affected, it is better to take a more empathetic approach, and instead, seek out how you can help and support, with questions like, 'Is something bothering you?' and 'What support do you need?'

We also have to remember that not everyone will know what help they need—even if they are aware that they do need support. As a line manager, once you've established that everyone is comfortable asking for help, the next questions to ask yourself are, 'Do I know how to provide this person with help?' and 'Do I have the resources to do so, and if not, do I know where to ask for those?'

Only then can you work through *how* you can best provide that support.

Taking the Long View

For all that, there are some actions that have a more immediate impact, many of the topics we discuss within DEI need to be considered from a generational perspective. We have to accept that progress can be slow and painful. Change takes time and it is about sustaining the small incremental steps that lead to a different reality for the next generation. What legacy do we want to leave? When we are clear on the outcome we want to achieve, it makes it much easier to work out what the next steps should be over shorter timescales.

It is easy to contemplate giving up when faced with obstacle after obstacle in your path. I have gone through many moments of self-doubt and wondered if I was making a difference. When you're in a leadership position, it is important to surround yourself with like-minded individuals, so that you can visibly and collaboratively work towards these ambitions—even if the outcome you want to see won't happen during your tenure.

We also need to know when to push and when to hold back. As leaders, we need to find the courage to make those decisions and be aware of when perhaps our organization could absorb more change. We have to find the balance between taking risks and playing it safe. It's not always an easy one to strike.

Donny had some fascinating insights on this point. 'When I think back to my time as a junior employee at Shell, I can see now that the assumptions I had about leaders and how they would perceive certain initiatives may not have been accurate. I bucked quite a few of my own assumptions when I was on the EC (Executive Committee).

'When I became a member of the EC, what I found was that when issues or opportunities were worked on, and then they percolated all the way up to the EC for a decision, by the time they reached us they'd sometimes be so watered down that they didn't always push enough. I can understand that people wanted to make it an easy decision for us, but having seen the approval process from both sides, I can confidently say that there were a lot of issues that the EC had a much greater risk appetite for than people lower down in the organization assumed.

'So, if you're lower down in the organizational hierarchy as you read this, I'd like to encourage you to think about how you could expand the boundaries of what could be. As leaders, we need to show our people that we don't just want safe options, we want ones that challenge the status quo. It can be easy to view a recommendation as "high risk" when you're looking at it in isolation, but the reality is that an executive team will be looking at it in the context of a much bigger picture, and what might seem high risk to you could actually present an acceptable risk to them.

'As senior leaders, we can provide the door for people to come to us with those more ambitious recommendations by creating a safe environment, where we demonstrate that we've got other people's backs. In my experience, by giving people a licence to operate on a broader envelope, you bring out the best in them. Therefore one of the most important questions that leaders can ask in their organizations is "What else?" How can you encourage people not to give you more of the same, but to instead look at how your organization can progress and develop?'

Tiny Rice Grains Contemplation

Explore: Look around your workplace and ask, what could we do better? Can you see any areas, no matter how small, that could be improved to make your workplace more inclusive?

Unpack: What else can you do? Is there any area where you can push for greater change and challenge the status quo?

Your reflections:

Know

....

....

Feel

....

....

Do

....

....

Part 2

Becoming More Curious

Curiosity is like a dance between two people. In a dance, there is a give and take. Both partners in it need to be connected. They need to trust one another, responding to what the other is doing, to ensure they can maintain the dance. Sometimes, they will step in sync, other times, they might separate, with each performing their own moves before coming back together. But they are both dancing to the same music and their intention is to work together to create a beautiful performance.

Curiosity is much the same. It, too, requires give and take. It's a dialogue between two people that leads to openness and change. Trust needs to be established between the two parties to give space to both for being vulnerable.

Whenever I don't know something in an area related to DEI, I have learned the best thing to do is to be curious and ask. For example, I don't know all the issues and experiences of those in the LGBTQ+ community. In my attempts to learn and better understand, I have turned to those who know this topic intimately, my LGBTQ+ colleagues. All I can do is be thankful to them for being so open and patient with me as I asked all the 'wrong' questions, and share that their reverse mentoring has been the most important when I've had to navigate dilemmas in this area.

We can all benefit from being more curious. In the context of DEI, this means we need to be open to hearing diverse views and experiences, all with the intent to impact change. One of the ways in which leaders can give everyone a voice is through employee resource groups (ERGS). ERGs provide a platform where leaders can collaborate to engage and drive change. It provides the opportunity to remove silos and integrate diverse perspectives.

We also have to find the courage to ask what can be uncomfortable questions, and to do so in such a way that we don't pass any judgement. This can be a challenging line to walk at times, but it is much easier when we approach life with the curiosity of a learner's mindset. This is crucial for learning about ourselves and by doing so, we then put ourselves in a better position to learn about others. This is why developing a learner's mindset is essential, and I'll cover this extensively in the next chapter.

Understanding others and demonstrating that we understand diverse perspectives and experiences is a powerful way to create engagement and to mobilize people to get behind positive change. Essentially, it is about culture building. Engagement at every level is crucial for DEI initiatives in any organization to succeed, and I've found the best way to develop that engagement is to be curious about how and what we can improve, so that we can share what we learn with others.

Chapter 6

Embracing a Learner's Mindset in DEI

In a general sense, the term 'learner's mindset' can be applied when an individual considers every new experience as an opportunity to learn. Those with a learner's mindset are open minded, and more agile in adapting to their surroundings.

This is particularly important given how quickly technology is changing the world around us. Research from Deloitte and the World Economic Forum in 2018 revealed that skills that once had a half-life of thirty years now have a half-life of just six years. That means the average person will need to reskill seven times during the course of their career.[13]

It is therefore essential that we help all of our employees develop a learner's mindset, because this will allow them to be agile, to learn and relearn new skills, and to stay ahead of the game in rapidly evolving workplaces. Similarly,

---

[13] Kemp, T. (2020) *The growth mindset: spurring a more skilled, engaged and innovative workforce.* Available at: https://www.forbes.com/sites/forbestechcouncil/2020/05/15/the-growth-mindset-spurring-a-more-skilled-engaged-and-innovative-workforce/?sh=425b917759ec

having a learner's mindset is also essential to move the DEI conversation forwards.

Jane Low, HR manager at Shell, knows this as well as anyone.

'What I've realized is that the values we hold and relationships we build in workplaces link very closely to the way we develop people in our talent programmes. When it comes to developing talent programmes that deliver results, it's important to build our curiosity muscles.

'I was involved in creating a program at Shell for Asian talent, for example, as well as a programme for women and one for LGBTQ+ talent. Although every group I've worked with has their differences, what I've also noticed is that there are commonalities across these talent development programmes, which is to draw the best out of the people in that group. This is interlinked with their diverse backgrounds and the strengths they bring.

'Part of my role when delivering these talent development programmes is to help those involved see what their strengths are and to see where they have blockers.'

Developing curiosity about yourself is therefore important in this context, otherwise it's hard to explore what your blockers might be and, more importantly, where they come from. This is when the curiosity that comes with a learner's mindset is crucial.

Jane explained that although the blockers can be similar across demographics, the reasons for those blockers are what vary from group to group—and to change behaviour and help unlock talent, each person needs to get to the heart of *why* they have that blocker before they'll be able to change it.

'For instance, in the context of Asia, one thing we often hear is that Asians are task-oriented and less adept at expressing their views and perspectives, and if views are expressed, it leans towards the "what" versus the "why". Therefore, one of the skills that can be developed is storytelling. However, I've been told this blocker is not unique to those from Asia only and can be similar for many people around the world. So, the key in developing a targeted development programme is to frame why that blocker exists in their context.

'In this situation, we can say that Asian people often prefer not to express their views, or if required will tend to discuss the "what" and "how", because of certain cultural norms, such as the hierarchical nature of most Asian societies. This desire to show respect to people who are more senior to us, alongside the desire for privacy, means we tend to draw a line between our private selves and our work selves. Modesty is an unspoken virtue in some Asian cultures, and for some people, talking too much about themselves might be considered inappropriate or even just irrelevant in the context of their work.

'However, this can be a blocker when it comes to giving feedback, particularly if they are being asked to give it to someone more senior to them. It might be construed as rude and disrespectful. So, part of our talent development programme focuses on how to do this respectfully, as well as helping them to understand the value behind giving feedback and in building trusted relationships. To develop this programme in a way that would help people and be meaningful to them, we had to adopt a mindset of curiosity to make sure we really understood where other people were coming from. Only then could we help them to see what their barriers were and how overcoming them would help them to bring their best selves to work and perform at a higher level.

'This is really important for organizations, as well as for individuals, because if people aren't able to bring their best selves to work then they will only bring half their capacity, creativity, and thinking. This isn't about making one group behave like another group, but about harnessing our differences and diversity, and bringing out the best in everyone as an outcome.'

Jane's point about understanding what is behind our blockers is interesting. Sometimes, people question whether talent programmes aimed at specific demographics—like women, the LGBTQ+ community, or ethnic groups—actually deepen divisions, rather than removing them. She's even asked that question herself, but having seen how these programmes work and the value they deliver, she's convinced that they reinforce relationships.

'I've thought very hard about why we offer programmes targeted at diverse groups rather than bringing everyone together. The key for me is that in such programmes, we are creating a safe space where we are able to go deeper into what different blockers mean to diverse groups.'

Reinforcing a Growth Mindset to Fuel a Learner's Mindset

Psychologist and researcher Carol Dweck is best known for defining the growth and fixed mindsets we all have. A growth mindset is slightly different to a learner's mindset, but to have one, you need the other. Those of us with primarily a growth mindset believe that our talents can be developed through hard work, good strategies, and input from others, whereas those of us with a more fixed mindset believe our talents are innate gifts. We all have a mix of growth and fixed mindsets, so our aim is to ensure that we fall into a growth mindset as often as possible.

Dweck's research shows that those with more of a growth mindset achieve more than those with more of a fixed one, and companies that embrace a growth mindset make their employees feel more empowered and committed.[14]

Within DEI, I believe that a growth mindset is important for developing and maintaining a learner's mindset. In individuals, this manifests as a willingness to learn from

[14] Harvard Business Review (2022) *What having a 'Growth mindset' actually means*. Available at: https://www.youtube.com/watch?v=r0qpJxEhOP4.

success and failures, and being open to new ideas, experiences, and perspectives. Organizations that demonstrate a growth mindset also receive greater support from their employees for collaboration and innovation—both of which, we know, are important for creating inclusive workplaces.

A growth mindset also encompasses the knowledge that you don't know everything or have all the answers. Being able to admit that requires a certain level of vulnerability—and to display that vulnerability, you need to feel psychologically safe to both admit you don't have all the answers and to be open to learning more. The kind of curiosity we need to open up conversations around DEI in a meaningful way, therefore, comes from having a growth mindset.

This all connects back to our intentions—understanding a situation from someone else's perspective is only valuable if we have the intention to grow as a result of having that new knowledge, and the intention to take action for positive change.

As I mentioned earlier, all of us need to develop a growth mindset, and by association, a learner's mindset, if we are to survive in the fast-paced modern world, where it's essential to update our skills and learn about new technologies and ways of working every few years if we are to remain relevant.

As articulated throughout the book, we know that diverse organizations are higher performing organizations. The research supporting this is compelling. We also know that to make progress in any area of DEI, there needs to be a set of standard expectations within the organization around what values are important to every member of the team.

To build high-performing teams, you need people with a growth mindset. Without a commitment to continuous learning, your teams will become stagnant, and those who do have a growth mindset will look for opportunities elsewhere, at companies that more actively encourage their development.

Leaders who role model a growth mindset will demonstrate the curiosity to open up those potentially uncomfortable conversations, to find the areas in which they can act to create a better environment for everyone.

This is one of the outcomes that Jane and her team want to see—and do see—from the talent development programmes.

'We've evolved the way we position these programmes and now we very much come at them from the perspective that they help every person on a team to learn and grow, but they can also help the team to work better together and understand how to bring out the best in each individual. When leaders came on our programmes, firstly we realized that they all had one part of themselves that, often unconsciously, they weren't bringing to work. And everyone wanted to have a safe space where they could talk about what that was for them.

'Secondly, through these programmes we were evoking curiosity and encouraging people to ask, "What can I learn now?" or "What can I learn to help me engage this person more?" Every leader should want to see the people on their team reaching their potential, and having these discussions has helped open up that curiosity about how to tap into each person's differences and strengths in a way that benefits everyone.

'One of the best things that has come from these programmes is helping more leaders realize that when they slow down and approach someone from a different background or with a different perspective with curiosity, they can build stronger, more open relationships. By showing they are curious and that they care, these leaders are able to engage better with their teams and tap into a level of discretionary effort that just wasn't there before.'

How Can You Be Curious? Who Do You Ask?

Within DEI, there can be a tendency to pass the challenges on to others: 'We don't have a problem here, because I've never been racist.'

'If the office isn't accessible for my colleague who has a disability, it's not my job to fix that, the organization should take care of it.'

'I'm supportive but we don't have the time or resources to deal with it now.'

These are some of the uncomfortable truths we have to deal with. It may be surprising to think that these thoughts or conversations still take place today. And they do. These are the mindsets that stop progress when people perceive an issue as one that belongs to someone else. Instead, we can help others move from a fixed mindset of, 'It's not my problem and I can't do anything,' to a growth mindset where they instead say, 'I don't know anything about this but I would be curious to learn more. How would I learn and what might I be able to do with that new knowledge?'

As Jane explained earlier, curiosity around our blockers is the key to helping more of us tap into a growth mindset. So, before we can be curious with others, we first need to be curious about ourselves.

Breaking Our Own Psychological Barriers

All of us will have 'fixed mindset triggers', which keep us from being curious, learning from mistakes and failures and embracing challenges. However, we all have 'growth mindset triggers' too.

One of the 'growth mindset triggers' that has served me well both personally and professionally, is my love of the great outdoors and high-altitude trekking. I started my first solo trekking trip about ten years ago, because I wanted to challenge myself physically and do something I had never done before. I chose Bhutan as the destination because it was the complete opposite of Singapore in terms of terrain: Singapore is an island and has a flat landscape, while Bhutan is landlocked and located in the Himalayan mountain range.

I had to overcome resistance from family and friends who questioned my decision to travel to a remote location on my own. I also had to become curious about Bhutan and its terrain, so I could plan my trip with sufficient knowledge and awareness. As I had never attempted high-altitude trekking on my own, I needed expert advice to plan for my trip as well. It also demanded physical fitness, which meant changing my daily habits. Eight months before my trip, I started training with an instructor and set fitness goals. Soon, I felt empowered, confident, and excited as I prepared and trained for my trek.

Since that first solo trip ten years ago, I have been on many other expeditions—both solo and with like-minded individuals—to many parts of the world covering four continents and counting! The outdoors and high-altitude trekking have also taught me perseverance and resilience, and about celebrating progress when things get tough (and I mean, *very* tough) at high altitude. It has also given me the chance to rely on others, to support others, and to work together to achieve a common goal. Travelling to remote locations and meeting people from all over the world with different cultures and backgrounds has also helped me to adopt a learner's mindset to embrace all that I don't know and can learn from. My travels have inspired me to be the best self I need to be outdoors, and these habits have also enriched me and made me a different leader at work.

My experience of taking up high-altitude trekking, and going on that first trip to Bhutan, illustrates some of the guiding principles you can use to help you become more curious about the world around you.

The first of these is to be curious without any judgement. When you form notions before you've learned anything, you kill your curiosity. So, if I had made judgements about Bhutan—such as I wouldn't have liked it because it's very different from Singapore, for the people are different and because the food is not to my liking; I'm only half joking when it comes to food, in Singapore most of us 'live to eat', whereas in Bhutan it's very much that you 'eat to live'—then I would have missed out an opportunity of a lifetime to discover and learn about another culture so different from mine, and to discover my love for adventures and mountain hiking.

The second principle is to know *why* you're curious about something or someone. We've all been in situations where someone else pretends they're interested in what we're saying, but we know that they don't really care and aren't being authentic. They are just asking questions for the sake of asking questions. If we start asking questions in relation to an area of DEI without knowing *why* we're curious about that area, the questions we ask will probably lead us down the wrong path.

There is a big difference between asking someone with a disability, for example, questions like, 'What help do you need to get your work done?', 'Is there any part of your day-to-day work that could be better supported?' or 'Could we provide some software that improves the way you work?' as opposed to asking questions like, 'Why were you born with this disability?' or 'How do you get on with your work?'

The first set of questions is framed with positive intent, where you're able to use your curiosity to make someone else's life better and more effective. By contrast, the second set of questions is not outcome focused and is judgement based. This ties into the third principle, which is about intentions. If you're curious because you genuinely want to make a difference, that will usually come through in the questions you ask.

In Chapter 2, I talked about the emotional tax that people from minority groups can pay when they are repeatedly asked about their experiences, particularly the negative ones. Curiosity is essential for us to understand one another, but we have to be mindful that the intentions behind our curiosity are good. We need to ensure that the conversations we initiate are focusing on moving the needle and making our workplaces better for everyone. Without having a clear intention and outcome in mind, we run the risk of going round in circles and having the same kinds of conversations over and over again, without making any kind of meaningful progress.

At the start of this chapter, I talked about the need for all of us to develop a learner's mindset. This state of mind requires curiosity and allows us to apply it in line with the principles I've just explained. There are other good reasons to develop a learner's mindset (and to encourage those around you to do the same). Studies show that those with a learner's mindset are more creative, innovative, and inclusive because they are more curious about other people's perspectives.[15]

I invite you to pause here and answer this question: Is there anything you've learned in your life that you're really proud of? Perhaps there is a skill that you thought you weren't good at but that you've now mastered? Maybe someone else told you that you wouldn't be able to master it and you proved them wrong. Or was there an achievement that seemed impossible but that became possible?

Think of that moment, whatever it is, and then answer this question: How did you feel and what did you learn? If you grew in that area of your life, can you see how you can grow in others?

---

[15] *Education systems can stifle creative thought. Here's how to do things differently* (2022). Available at: https://www.weforum.org/agenda/2018/04/education-systems-can-stifle-creative-thought-here-s-how-to-do-things-differently/

Tiny Rice Grains Contemplation

Explore: How have you built micro habits that have served you to push through in areas that are new to you? Where have you learned what's possible?

Unpack: How have you demonstrated an unwavering commitment to learn, share, and grow as you mature and evolve in your leadership journey? Who do you reach out to and how do you consciously build a network which will help you grow?

Your reflections:

Know

....

....

Feel

....

....

Do

....

....

Chapter 7

The Power of Engagement

In 2020, I was working with my DEI team on implementing our refreshed strategy. After months of working on our plans, I was talking to my external adviser, Natalie, who was my sounding board. She asked, 'Lyn, I have one question, how did this come about?'

I explained that we had engaged with staff at every level of the organization, representatives from the various ERGs and from different countries, because we wanted to make sure we heard the global perspective and considered all the different cultures that make up our organization. The ERGs were particularly important, because they provide the channel to build shared goals, relationships, and trust. But while the ERGs help deliver the organizational strategy, it is leaders who own the accountability and because we know that people who feel valued are more engaged, we wanted to ensure everyone felt heard and that their contribution was valued. I was proud that the work we were implementing involved so many people and represented a diversity of perspectives.

Natalie listened. Then, she said, 'It's important that you communicate how this came about when you implement this new strategy. People need to know and be reminded that this didn't come about from just you and a few team members, but that this strategy came out of the company's collective voice.'

Natalie taught me an important lesson: engagement provides an avenue to involve and incorporate diverse voices. It creates pride and gives individuals a sense of shared purpose and joint accountability for DEI. In addition, visibly sharing the outcomes of these engagements goes a long way in reinforcing what being curious can lead to.

It is easy to connect with—and therefore engage—someone when you are able to have a one-to-one conversation with them. But how can you recreate that atmosphere and environment to engage people in a global setting? It's a challenge we have to tackle as leaders in global organizations. How can we still create the connection necessary for strong engagement, without speaking to everyone individually?

I am not an engagement or a communications expert by any means. We all have a different style of engagement. If you're a leader, you will have likely found a style that you're comfortable with and has worked for you. Perhaps, you're starting to experiment with other engagement styles for different audiences. My intent, therefore, is not to tell you how to engage, but to share with you what has worked for me. Hopefully, it can serve as a prompt for you to reflect on what your engagement style is.

Like you, I have had my fair share of failures and successes when it comes to engagement, be it public speaking or written communications. I've engaged one-on-one, with small groups, and with big audiences. I've evolved from shying away from public speaking to feeling comfortable and confident when I have to engage with audiences of varied sizes and demographic groups.

Here are some engagement principles I have worked on:

1. *Listen to understand versus listening to reply.*[16] When I am listening to understand, I put the person I am engaging with at the centre of the engagement. In doing this, I have to demonstrate empathy, curiosity, and care in what is being shared with me. I pick up the nuances of what is said and not said. This helps to build trust in engagement.

   Listening to reply can sometimes come across as intellectual and impersonal. Have you ever received a response to your question/inquiry and your immediate

[16] Zenger, J. (2021) *What great listeners actually do.* Available at: https://hbr.org/2016/07/what-great-listeners-actually-do.

reaction was, 'Is this from a template?' or 'Is this scripted'? Did you feel like you had not been heard?

2. *Be mindful and connect deeply with your audience.* Marc Lesser[17] developed the seven practices of a mindful leader and has taught these practices to leaders at some of the world's biggest companies. He acknowledges that while the seven practices are simple to understand, they can be challenging to embody in day-to-day life. These seven practices are:
    i. Love the work of being mindful.
    ii. Do the work, by which he means develop a regular meditation and mindfulness practice.
    iii. Don't be an expert. This one particularly resonates with me, because it speaks to the need to approach our lives and challenges with an open mind, and the ability to let go of always being right.
    iv. Connect to your pain is another practice that I feel is important. He is talking about learning from your own experiences, especially those that hurt, and taking the time to reflect on what those experiences were and how they have made you feel.
    v. Connect to the pain of others, which I feel embodies what we've been talking about around

[17] Inam, H. (2019) *The Seven Practices of Mindful Leaders.* Available at: https://www.forbes.com/sites/hennainam/2019/06/25/the-seven-practices-of-mindful-leaders/

curiosity. This is about openly listening to others and not avoiding the uncomfortable truths that might come out of difficult conversations.

vi. Depending on others is another of the practices that particularly resonates with me, because it refers to building caring communities and developing deeper connections with others.

vii. Keep making it simpler is the final practice. Lesser's advice with this one is to always ask, 'What is most important right now?' and then to do that.[18]

3. *Be humble and build trust.* Humble leaders focus their actions outward and seek to improve team performance, not just individual performance. They channel their ambition back into the organization, rather than towards themselves. They build a culture of psychological safety based on trust, openness, and recognition; and by modelling behaviour, they foster a culture of development and encourage learning and growth.[19]

4. *Be consciously inclusive.* If you are not consciously including, you are unconsciously excluding. In

---

[18] Inam, H. (2019) *The Seven Practices of Mindful Leaders*. Available at: https://www.forbes.com/sites/hennainam/2019/06/25/the-seven-practices-of-mindful-leaders/

[19] Robinson, E. (2024) *How humble leaders create engagement*. Available at: https://www.hoganassessments.com/blog/how-humility-creates-engagement-humble-leaders-build-trust/

engagements and communications, be sure to seek feedback and input from a diverse group of people so that it is representative of the cross section of your organization. This ensures that everyone feels included and valued, along with a sense of belonging.

Using conscious inclusion to escape from majority bias

Developing that muscle of conscious inclusion is particularly important if you are part of the majority where you live or work. When you are in that 'majority' group, you are often unaware of the obstacles which others may encounter.

What is your style of engagement? Who do you get feedback from to improve your engagement? What are your strengths? What are the aspects you want to improve on?

Engaging through Networks and Alliances

One of the best ways that I have found to engage with others at a large organization is through employee resource groups (ERGs). These are networks of people with shared goals and common purpose to build inclusion in the workplace. For example, in many organizations, there are ERGs for gender balance, ones which work on creating safer and more inclusive workplaces for those in the LGBTQ+ community, and those who advocate for improving accessibility within workplaces and communities for those with disabilities, to name a few.

These groups give everyone, regardless of their position in the organizational hierarchy, an opportunity to lead in an area they're passionate about.

The ERGs are successful because they come together based on common values and mindsets. They are clear about their purpose and everyone involved is passionate about this cause. These topics are too big to be tackled by any of us as individuals, so groups such as these provide a collaborative platform and create huge networks of people with different skills and talents.

What I've learned in my years of working within the DEI space is that it's not everyone doing the same thing that leads to change: it's everyone leveraging their abilities, doing different things, but with a shared goal and common purpose that delivers the most impactful change. When we are able to bring people together and have this diversity of perspectives, we can create a bigger voice and achieve more, together. Essentially, it is about culture building.

Collaboration is at the heart of why these ERGs are successful. I talked earlier about Marc Lesser's seven practices of mindful leaders, and I feel three of those are particularly relevant in this context: Don't be an expert, connect to the pain of others, and depend on others. For example, I'm a big picture person. I can visualize how I want something to look, but I'm not always the right person to operationalize that vision.

I love documentaries, especially biographical films and hearing other people's stories, as they always seem to get right to my heart. So, I prefer approaching engagement from this perspective. Earlier in Chapter 2, I discussed how I had introduced deliberate 'positive disruptions' in the organization to enable individuals to have a more intentional response to DEI instead of being on autopilot (System 1 versus System 2 thinking).

With this objective, I wanted to create a series of films that were more personal and emotive, which shared and confronted real people's stories and experiences. While this was my vision, I couldn't execute it alone. For one thing, I didn't have the creative talent, nor the technical expertise of a filmmaker. But I also wanted people to come forward with their stories, so my team and I reached out to our ERGs. The strength of that network meant there were lots of ideas about what these stories should be.

Then I had to depend on others—a team of talented creatives who could translate my vision for these short films and bring it to life. They did a fantastic job and went on to create a series of award-winning biographical films titled *Unique People, Powerful Together*—one of the awards it won was the Cannes Corporate Media and TV Awards.

Michael Massey, the filmmaker who led the project, reflected on how making the DEI films had opened his eyes and mind.

'At the start of the project, I genuinely questioned what I'd be able to contribute. Was I even the right person for the job? In retrospect, that "naivety" was my strength. During research, as I listened to the stories of those willing to openly share their experiences, I realized that if I could take viewers on this same journey of learning, using film to translate the emotions that I was feeling, then we had a real opportunity to make a difference. I'm grateful to all those who were brave enough to take part. It is their truthful, powerful stories that are the real engine of this film, helping to educate and inspire us to show up.'

But I could never have done this alone, I needed the creativity and passion of many others to pull this together. This whole project was not about me, but about us, as a collective.

There are some guiding principles that I have found helpful when setting up ERGs, particularly in a global organization where you will often have many of such networks. The first of these is to provide structure and support to guide those in individual ERGs on what to work on. This comes down to prioritization and making sure that the organization's priorities are clearly communicated to these networks.

Secondly, leaders have to decide what resources the organization will provide for those who are passionate about a cause. In many cases, ERG leads have common interest and passion, but they may not have the right connection to leaders who are allies and who want to sponsor, mentor, and champion initiatives by the ERGs.

Thirdly, it is also helpful to provide a formal structure to channel people's passion. This allows the informal and the formal to work together in a way that leads to success.

Finally, as leaders we can provide skills and support people's development as we see them evolving and emerging as leaders within these groups and networks. It is good to ask ourselves what the person needs to be successful, so that overall they can contribute to the success of the organization. What support, skills, development, or exposure can you provide to help them? How can you guide them so that they can find clarity about the impact they want to have and the support they need?

You never know where this kind of support might take someone. Sometimes, it can lead to positive impacts far beyond your organization, as Vishal's experience shows. He is now involved in setting up a social inclusion accelerator programme in India, which supports start-ups that are creating solutions for people with disabilities.

'It all started from the thought that there are so many day-to-day independent living challenges that people with all kinds of different disabilities face, but that there are not enough solutions or products to tackle them,' Vishal explained.

'I was talking to start-ups that were having difficulties sustaining what they were creating because the number of people with specific disabilities they could reach was limited. They were disconnected from that world and didn't know how to tap into it. But these start-ups were doing something phenomenal, because they were moving from a charity mindset to a higher-demand model. This is much more sustainable because if you see this community as a customer segment it can sustain a business.

'However, what we realized was that the biggest challenge for the entrepreneurs behind these start-ups was the time it was taking to break even and achieve profitability. It was taking longer because it takes them longer to find their customers who are typically lower-volume markets. There were also no economies of scale, which can make affordability an issue. Ultimately, there were two main challenges: the high cost of product and low awareness level.

'Through this accelerator programme, we are supporting start-up entrepreneurs financially and through mentorship, along with connecting them to a network of people with disabilities and to relevant investors. It's still at a nascent stage, but we're already starting to see the impact it's having.

'For example, we're working with one company that is using AI to create a product to help people with hearing and speech impairment communicate more easily. One of the challenges people who communicate with sign language face is that many people don't know sign language. So, this product takes their signs and translates them into audio, which someone who doesn't know sign language can hear. They can speak in response, and what they say will be translated into text that the other person can read.'

This is a remarkable example of how engaging with others and collaborating through networks can lead to improvements in people's lives. As Vishal told me, it's all about focusing your efforts in the right place. 'When we can find the parts of the ecosystem that are transforming accessibility and inclusion efforts, and focus our attention there, we can accelerate the whole DEI journey.'

Vishal, and everyone else who is involved in this accelerator programme, have found incredible ways to spread their influence further, and create tangible impacts as a result—all by focusing on the very human challenges they are in a position to help solve.

Focusing on the Human

When we make our work around DEI focused on the human experience, the response is heartfelt because we all have a story. We can all think of times when we have been excluded, and we all have moments when we feel included, valued and feel a deep sense of belonging. We will all be able to share times when we've felt really proud of what we've achieved or how we've behaved.

These human experiences and stories are one of the most powerful ways to build engagement around DEI strategies across a diverse global workforce. It levels the playing field and focuses us on what is the most important—that we all have different and diverse stories to tell, and if we consciously and mindfully engage from this perspective, we build true inclusion where everyone feels respected, valued, and a sense of belonging.

When we have the courage to say, 'I don't know but I want to learn,' we demonstrate our curiosity to learn, make mistakes, and ask for help when we need it. It can be helpful to keep coming back to the intent behind our curiosity. Ask yourself, why do I want to learn about this topic? How can I have a positive impact on others by discovering more about this area?

When we focus on being curious from a place of caring about others, it helps us to take responsibility for making a positive change. What I've found is that the more we role model caring curiosity, the more we empower other people within our organizations to do the same. Perhaps you've noticed this too? This all helps build a groundswell of support for DEI strategies because everyone in the organization can see and feel the positive impact.

As I explained in the previous chapter, one of the foundational elements of building a movement of positive change is helping everyone in your organization develop a growth and learner's mindset to enable all of us to approach learning from an authentic perspective, with an open mind.

It is invaluable to have a vision we can all work towards creating. The vision we set as leaders can help others prioritize their activities and even if people across the organization are working on different things, they are all working towards a shared goal.

How Mindfulness Supports Our Vision for the Future

I talked earlier about the seven practices for mindful leaders, but I've found that mindfulness is a valuable tool that can help us when we are creating a vision for the future. When we are mindful of the present, it grounds us on visualizing how it could be different in the future.

It's important to remember that DEI is a growth journey. This is work that will continue for generations and will evolve as social expectations shift and change. When we explicitly talk about the world we want to leave for the next generation, for our children, grandchildren, and all those who are close to us, we create an emotional connection to the vision we have. Vishal is an excellent example of someone with an emotional connection to a vision of a more inclusive future. He is using his passion to drive engagement both within the organization he works for and outside it, and as a result, is making progress that has a positive impact on many people.

Tiny Rice Grains Contemplation

Explore: What is your style of engagement and who do you get feedback from to improve your engagement?

Unpack: How would you like the future to look? What areas do you need to be more curious about? Who can you ask to help you better understand the present and plot a course to that vision of the future?

Your reflections:

Know

....

....

Feel

....

....

Do

....

....

Part 3

Caring About Humanity

Care is an attribute present in every meaningful discussion around DEI because, at the heart of it, it is the intention to create a place of belonging—one where everyone feels included. We want people to feel free to be themselves at work, and to know that their unique perspectives are valued by their colleagues and the organizations they work for. We want everyone to feel cared for and, in turn, to care for those around them.

Caring for ourselves, for those around us and for humanity as a whole, is integral to this theme of belonging and well-being. However, for care to be felt, it has to be intentional, consistent, and other-focused. Often, the concept of care is linked only to our emotions and how we feel. Instead, I would suggest care can also be considered from a more systemic and consistent point of view. What we want to achieve is wholehearted care. But what does this look like?

Vishal shared a wonderful example from his onboarding at Shell, which to my mind, shows what wholehearted care can look like when it is embedded within an organization as a whole.

'I had the most delightful joining experience. When I was called for an interview for a role at Shell, I told them about my disability [being visually impaired]. Before that interview, the DEI lead called me to understand my accommodation needs so they could make sure that the interview and selection process was inclusive. That wasn't something I'd even really thought of before it happened.

'Of course, when I went for my interview I had some assistance, but otherwise, the process was just as it was for anyone else. Once I accepted the offer of a job, my experience became even better and went beyond what I could have imagined. I was invited for a workplace accessibility assessment, which took place on one day. During that time, I spoke to a doctor, so the company could understand my health and safety context and ensure a support system was set up accordingly. I spoke to the IT manager who understood assistive technology to make sure I had the technology I needed, like a screen reader set up on my laptop.

'I also met with the facility manager and DEI lead, who took me through the office space I would be working in to understand how to manage it and how to access what I needed. They captured any requirements I had during this visit including, for example, the fact that the coffee machine was a touchscreen that I could not see, so they added braille to it for me.

'They also provided door-to-door transportation to ensure my commute was safe. Before I joined, they also did some training with my team, so that they would know how to do things like make documents accessible for me. They ran through some basic dos and don'ts with everyone so that, by the time I started, everything was set. The granularity they went to in order to make my onboarding as smooth as possible was incredible.'

To me, this shows care at every level of the organization: from the policies and procedures in place to the way in which individuals on various teams interacted with and welcomed Vishal into his new role. Of course, you've already heard from Vishal in this book about how he continues to pay that care and kindness forward to others.

Can you imagine how it would feel if everyone in your organization felt that cared for?

Chapter 8

Wholehearted Care

My dogs, Bailey and Fuji, are my best friends, and also my inspiration for what I define as 'wholehearted care'. Whether I step outside to empty the garbage, go for a fifteen-minute journey to the gas station, or stay away from home for three weeks, the greeting I get from my dogs every time I return is always the same. I know I'll be welcomed home at the front door, with excitement, licks, and lots of affection. Their love and loyalty for me is wholehearted. I treat them with love, respect, and care, and they treat me the same way. My dogs make me feel like I belong.

Earlier in the book, I discussed how there can be physical barriers that can affect our ability to do our work, or even just participate in simple activities in an office, like making a morning cup of coffee. If you use a wheelchair, for instance, can you enter through the front door, or do you need to use an alternative entrance at the back of the building where the service lift is? Can you reach the cupboards and kitchen surfaces to make your own cup of coffee?

Do you have to struggle to get things done? Do you have the tools you need to make your days productive or do you have to fight to get the support you need? All of these seemingly small things create barriers to inclusion.

When the organization cares unconditionally, there are policies and processes to ensure that the workplace is inclusive. However, to sustain this as a culture, it needs the leaders to role model what this looks like and to be on the lookout for those barriers and do all that we can to remove them. Take Vishal's story as an example: every leader he encountered did what they could to identify and remove barriers for him. This care rippled out into his team, and has since, gone even further.

Start With Yourself

Before we can care for others though, we have to care for ourselves. But the practice of self-care can be tricky for leaders in particular to embrace. It can feel selfish to take time out for ourselves and it can leave us wondering how we can care for others if we're putting ourselves first. Feeling guilty about caring for ourselves can mean we say no to doing so. But it's crucial that we introduce care for ourselves into our lives.

Olga, who shared her story about inclusive recruitment earlier in the book, knows this better than anyone. When her son was around eight years old, he lost his hearing in one ear. She remembers finding it challenging to adapt as a parent.

'It happened quite suddenly and I had a difficult time adjusting. Sometimes, I felt it was more difficult for me than it was for my son. My husband and I had all these big questions: How will it affect his studies? His relationship with friends? His life? But there were also all the little practical things: like, when he went to bed and was lying on his good ear, and I would come into his bedroom to say goodnight, he wouldn't react because he couldn't hear me. Or if we were walking along talking, it would sometimes take me a few minutes to realize that he wasn't engaging with the conversation because I was walking on the side of his bad ear.

'He also didn't want to tell anyone about his hearing problem. I remember when he was getting ready to go back to school that he didn't want people to know and think differently of him. I found that a lot of the training I'd received through work about accessibility and managing this kind of situation was really helpful. But one of the most important things I realized was that I couldn't give what I didn't have. And that meant that I needed to show kindness to myself through this process first, because otherwise I wouldn't have been able to show enough kindness to him. I needed to make sure I was okay, so that I could authentically help and care for him in the way he needed me to on this journey.

'When he lost his hearing, I remember going through a whole palette of emotions. I was anxious, scared, worried. Happy, when we finally found the cause. Devastated, when we learned it was permanent. You name it, I went through it. As a mother, of course, you want the best for your child. Even though his condition was not life threatening, my mind would supply all kinds of scenarios of where things could go wrong because of his hearing loss—like him crossing the street and not hearing the car coming. That wasn't particularly helpful, and I knew that I needed to make peace with it, so that I could focus on what was really important, which, of course, was making sure he was okay.

'I knew I needed help from people around me to accept it. I would lean on my husband, although I was often mindful not to use him as an emotional waste bin with everything going on. I had a really good group of friends who I could talk to, as well as my sisters. It was important for me to have people I could turn to and say, "Oh my god, I'm freaking out," because even just that process of voicing what had been playing on my mind helped me process things. Then, I would listen to another perspective and that helped a lot too. Having that support structure was invaluable and helped me care for myself so that I could be there for my son.'

As Olga demonstrated, when we care for ourselves, we are ensuring we can be the best we possibly can and we can extend more care to others. We are taking the time to build resilience and prevent burnout so that we can thrive and perform at work. However, blocking out personal time in our diaries, particularly as leaders, can feel like a selfish act, even if it benefits not only us but also our teams.

We have to challenge this internal narrative and remind ourselves of the power of kindness. Often, in a work context, being kind can be seen as being 'soft', or even 'unprofessional'. What I have come to realize is that we can't be the best at any part of our jobs if we can't practice kindness towards ourselves.

Kindness towards ourselves looks different for each of us, but I invite you to take a moment now to think about what it looks like for you. If you're being kind to yourself, how do you start your day? What is the first thing that you do to prepare for all the other things that you need to take care of? I find it helps to remember that giving yourself the time and space to prepare for your day ahead can mean that you can be better for someone else.

The Challenge of Showing Kindness to Ourselves

This idea of taking time to care for yourself, so as to better care for others, might sound like a no-brainer to some of you reading this. Personally, it took me by surprise when I realized I didn't always practise kindness towards myself. It felt like a strange concept when I first started thinking about how I was showing unkindness towards myself, and how that could impact others as a result.

As leaders we cannot take kindness and self-care for granted. Showing kindness to ourselves is difficult. Making sure that we don't set unrealistic expectations for ourselves that we can never meet is important. This also reflects on how we behave with others, because our kindness for ourselves is our benchmark for the kindness that we show others.

When Jane and I spoke, she described how she shows more kindness to herself and escapes from a negative emotional spiral. Perhaps, some of what Jane shared with me will resonate with you too.

'Showing kindness for myself has been difficult at times. I have gone through negative emotional cycles of thinking "I didn't do this well," "I didn't say that right," and "I didn't give the best impression of that . . .' The thing that I found helped me stop those cycles was to ask myself "If I told someone else about this and they helped me process it, did it really happen the way I think it did? Did my actions or words really contribute to a negative impression or outcome? Was that real?" Often what I would realize was that the situation was nowhere near as negative as I had imagined.

'I've also noticed that if I'm being overly critical of other people, that is a sign that I'm being harsh to myself too. When I realize I'm thinking this way, I check in and ask myself, "What's my well-being state?" To counter any negativity, I focus on important self-identity messages that speak to who I really am. Often, this is the reverse of what I'm criticizing myself for—I'm equipped. I'm able. I have insights. I have strengths. I have gifts and wisdom to impart to people.

'When self-doubt creeps in, it can really shake my core because it comes from very deep-seated feelings, so I question it to help remove it. I don't lean too hard towards kindness, but I know that when I question these doubts and centre myself, kindness comes through for myself and for others. When I do this, I can look at the others around me and know that there is more room for me to be able to see where other people are coming from and therefore show kindness and compassion for where they're at.'

Jane makes an excellent point. Think about this honestly—if you are relentless with yourself, you will probably be the same with others. If we have had to struggle to get where we are, there is a mistaken belief that those coming through behind us should also have to struggle. We wear it like a badge of honour, telling ourselves that it's good to be hard on ourselves, because that's what it takes to succeed in life.

So ask yourself now, Are you happy with your own level of self-care? If yes, why? If you're not, why not? What could you do differently?

None of this is rocket science. It's likely not groundbreaking for those of you reading this. But it is about habit forming and prioritizing self-care. I know I frequently get distracted and forget to care for myself because I start my day in a rush.

We can feel like we're being buried under the weight of expectations to be a carer, an employee, a leader, and on top of all the roles we have in our lives, to make time to have fun. With so many competing priorities for our time, it can be easy to go through the day without checking in on ourselves. We have to start there—asking ourselves how we are feeling and whether we feel cared for. Or, as Jane put it, asking ourselves what is my well-being state?

When I took some time out of work because I was on the verge of burnout in 2023, I felt incredibly guilty about my workload falling on the other people in my team. A really good friend, Carlos Maurer, helped me to see that focusing on my own self-care wasn't selfish. In fact, the opposite was true. Not taking time to care for myself would be worse not only for me, but also for my team.

Carlos listened as I offloaded about the guilt I was feeling for taking time out. Then he said, 'When you think about it Lyn, it's good that you feel guilt, because you're human. It's good that you have empathy around the impact this is having on your team and what they have to bear in terms of resources being spread more thinly. But you also have to remember this is not all on you. This is also about the resources available within the organization, and about different choices being made about work priorities to support your team too, this doesn't all fall on your shoulders.'

Life happens. People will go on sick leave, take maternity or paternity leave, or need time off for any number of reasons. At an organizational level, there need to be policies and embedded values and mindsets that allow for people to feel psychologically safe to take time out when they most need it.

Carlos' words didn't solve the problem immediately and, of course, I still felt guilty, but he gave me a different perspective on the issue. He helped me see that I didn't have to hold on and not show care for myself because I was worried about passing the problem to someone else.

By taking the time to listen to me, he also gave me an opportunity to talk, feel better, and gain new insight. I was able to think about how to prioritize the work I was leaving for my team: How much of it needed to be done and what could wait? Who could do the tasks that were a priority and what help could we get from elsewhere in the organization to facilitate that?

Care in Action

It's not enough to say that we care, whether about our colleagues or the organization we work for. We have to move beyond just saying, 'I care,' or, 'Take care of yourself,' as throwaway platitudes. We have to demonstrate 'care' by our actions.

Caring at an appropriate level is an artform. Executing it well doesn't fit into a neat box. The fundamental ways in which we can show we care are firstly to listen to those around us and understand what they need. Do not assume what others' needs are.

Secondly, we have to show curiosity. We can only truly care about someone if we know who they are and their individual circumstances. We have to form human relationships with those we lead so that we can truly show up for others in moments of need.

When we put the concept of caring into the context of DEI, it helps to create an environment that allows people to do their best work. The intention is to build care into the organization, through its policies, practices, behaviours, and mindsets of leaders and all staff members.

As leaders, if we are more centred, grounded, and clearer about our intentions, it's very likely that we'll have the positive impact we're seeking on those who we lead. We will be role modelling what it looks like to care for ourselves and, by extension, to care for others. If the groups we lead take this on board and do the same, it has a ripple effect.

One person who knows more about the ripple effect than most is Simon Leow, co-founder of the Happiness Initiative, which he established to help people master happiness after going on his own journey of discovery to uncover what made him happy. We heard from him briefly in Chapter 2.

'Many years ago, I was severely depressed, so I went to see a psychiatrist. In our first appointment, he suggested I take medication, but after asking him about the potential side effects I wasn't convinced that was the route for me. This was when he suggested that, as I was still very rational, I could talk through my problems in sessions. But then he said something I did not expect. "So Simon, your friend recommended you to me and I know you are out of a job now, so I'm not sure you could afford the fee for consultations."

'I was taken aback. I asked how much each session would cost, to which he replied around $300. When I asked how many sessions he thought I'd need, he told me around twenty.

'Although I told him I'd be able to afford that with my savings, when I stepped out of that consulting room I felt lousy. At the reception, the nurse asked when I wanted my next appointment and I replied, "Let me think about it."

'As I walked out of the psychiatrist's office and along the street, I saw a sign for a Singapore Airlines office and I stepped inside. By the time I left, I had an open-ended ticket to France in my pocket. Three days later, I was on a plane. I'd always had an adventurous spirit—when I was at university I backpacked around China for sixty days. But somehow, when I got into work, I lost my connection to the things that I loved to do—like travelling. One of the reasons I'd left my job was because I'd realized it had made me lose my connection with my freedom and creativity.

'Sometimes in life we can get drawn deeper and deeper into something—like climbing the corporate ladder at work—without realizing that it's drawing us away from the things we love. It's easy to think that there's a light at the end of the tunnel and that things will get better, but if you didn't resonate with what you were doing in the first place, climbing higher up the corporate ladder won't do anything to help you.'

Simon's experience of travelling at this point in his life, when he felt depressed and was unsure of what direction to take fascinated me, but I'm sure many of us can relate to a sense of losing connection with the things that we love.

'Being in a completely different location, with a different culture, language, and food, turned out to be exactly what I needed. Now, I'm not suggesting that everyone who is depressed should avoid treatment and travel instead, but in my experience, when I was in Singapore, everywhere I went to evoked a depressive memory. I don't think that staying there would have been helpful for me, but I hadn't expected travelling to be so transformative for my mental health.

'When I look back now, I can see that it was the interruption of my thought patterns and behaviours, along with all the new stimuli, that was particularly helpful for me. After spending three months in western Europe, I decided I wanted to see Asia, so I booked a ticket to Thailand. Here, I found work in exchange for accommodation and food in a village, and I spent the next three months in Thailand, learning a new language and getting used to this new culture.

'I left Thailand to return to Singapore, where I worked in a café and got into education consultancy as a freelancer. I was still travelling, and it was on one of my trips in 2013 that I had my eureka moment. I was standing in a queue in a bakery in Germany and all the staff looked so grouchy. I started wondering why, and then I saw it: I think people want to be happy, but they just don't know how to express it! Immediately, I went online and searched "mastering happiness".

'That led me to the Masters in Applied Positive Psychology at the University of Pennsylvania. I started my course in 2014, and this was when I realized there was a whole movement around taking psychological science and using it to improve people's well-being. Instead of seeing people as problems, we were seeing how we could make the best out of the human condition and I was fascinated.

'One of my fellow alumni started running short certification programmes in applied positive psychology at a small institution on the other side of Philadelphia from the campus. One weekend, they invited me to come down to attend one of them. Initially, I couldn't understand why anyone would pay for such a certification, when there was such a prestigious university offering a full course nearby. Soon, I realized that the fact it was shorter and cheaper must have appealed to many people (I'd been living on a budget of $10 a day while studying, so I knew my master's wasn't cheap!). But the most interesting part of this experience was seeing the community come together to learn about well-being. It stayed in the back of my mind.

'When I returned to Singapore in 2015, I started trying to promote positive psychology but no one here had heard of it, and well-being wasn't a topic anyone was talking about. Soon, I went back to my freelance consultancy work. But two years later, my friend Sherman (who became the co-founder of the Happiness Initiative with me) left his job and finally read a book, *The Resilience Factor*, which I had been recommending to him for years. He was fascinated by the scientific approach to how our beliefs can make us more resilient, and he wanted to do something with it. I'd been wanting to do something to make well-being more accessible to more people for years.

'So, we started the Happiness Initiative with the objective of preventing people from getting trapped in the downward spiral I had found myself in a few years before.

'I realized that my mental health condition hadn't appeared overnight. While it was a long and insidious process that put me into a downward spiral, a trigger had worsened it quickly. Of course, there can be risk factors that can also set you on this path—like a family history of depression—but it is still a journey to the bottom of that spiral. My aim was to find a way to interject at different points in people's lives and to take a more preventative approach towards preventing mental health conditions from developing and to build well-being.

'I started the Happiness Initiative because I believe that even when people are not "unwell" they still benefit from focusing on their well-being and should they later become unwell, they will have some skills to help them navigate the experience.'

Simon's story demonstrates why we need to make time for our own self-care and underscores the importance of care from others to help us focus on our well-being, if we slip into a downward spiral. His experience and work through the Happiness Initiative demonstrates that sometimes it's just one small action that can make the difference—a tiny rice grain or a drop in the ocean that leads to ever-expanding ripples.

Stepping Into Being

Like dropping a single rice grain into water creates ripples, small acts of kindness and inclusion can have ripple effects, inspiring others to do the same and creating a cascading impact for those around us. Each of our small actions adds up to a greater whole. Sometimes, we can get disheartened if we don't see others doing their part, or if we can't see how what we're doing will make a difference. However, we need to approach this from a different angle—one of *being* versus *doing*.

When we are present in our interactions, we can be centred, grounded, and be fully available to the situation or the person we are dealing with. This is why I find having a mindfulness practice so helpful, because it encourages us to be present. We spend so much of our lives being distracted, rather than being present, but often it is the simple act of being there for another person that makes all the difference.

Jane made a similar observation during our conversation. 'Sometimes, I've realized that care is just about being there for people. I don't have to be saying a lot or doing a lot, just my presence in itself is enough.'

She also revealed that she has found it helpful to put herself in other people's positions, so that she can be compassionate when they are struggling.

'I recently had an interaction with a colleague that was quite negative. I picked up some strong signals that they didn't think I was confident in my job and their body language was almost aggressive. But I also knew that this individual was going through a difficult time and I thought that if I were in their position, I would probably be angry too. That allowed me to have a lot more compassion for them and, even though their behaviour was quite negative, I could let it go.

'For me, kindness has to come from a place where you think well of the other person, and where you have the highest regard for them. Sometimes, it has to be very intentional, but I believe we also need to know where our kindness and compassion are coming from, to ensure they're genuine, and that we are giving the other person what they need, whether it's support or space.'

It can help to think about your intention for each interaction and what outcome you are hoping for. Before you speak, think about your intention. This might sound laborious and clunky, but it's a micro habit that will lead to a change if you practise it enough over time. Your intention can be as simple as having a conversation based on mutual respect, or to gain something by giving to the other person, or even to come away from an interaction feeling as though it was positive for both you and the other person involved.

Remember that the outcome we are ultimately looking for, by developing this habit of wholehearted care, is a sense of belonging and inclusion. We want everyone to feel they are part of the team, fully contributing and being their best selves at work.

As leaders we set the tone for what is and isn't accepted within our teams and wider organizational communities. We also set the expectations for how the company's values translate into the values of our teams. Therefore, we have to consider what behaviours are valued and reinforced versus not.

For example, do you always reward the highest performer, even if they demonstrate non-inclusive behaviours? If a leader does not set the standards for acceptable versus unacceptable behaviours, then it would not surprise you that the work culture is not inclusive.

Therefore, we have to think carefully about the behaviours we reward and what impact that will have on the team as a whole, and on the culture we are trying to build. Sometimes, this can mean having difficult conversations, but they make all the difference. As Jane explained to me though, when you come from a place of care, delivering feedback is always better than staying silent.

'I think it's important for leaders to tell people when they are falling short in terms of their performance, because in doing so you're helping them. I truly believe everyone wants to do a better job, so if you also believe that then by giving someone direct, honest feedback, you will get their attention and help them improve.

'When I give direct feedback, I always set the foundation and tell them that I'm saying this because I really care, and because it is important for both them and me. I don't want to hide anything and I think it's essential to have these honest conversations to support the members of my team and myself to do better.

Whenever I've taken this approach to sharing feedback, it is never a difficult conversation, because we both understand one another and know it's coming from a place of care.

'I know that giving feedback can be something a lot of leaders struggle with, but I've found that viewing it through this lens of care helps to shift the focus away from the task and onto people. It is people who get the tasks done, so I would say that if leaders can shift their focus onto people, they will find it easier to share negative feedback with their team members, because they will understand that it is coming from a position of care. It's all about approaching these conversations with the right intent, from a place of relationship building and trust.'

I love that Jane has reframed giving feedback, both negative and positive, as a process through which you can show care. Have you struggled with giving honest feedback to others in the past? Do you think taking this perspective might help you when you're delivering feedback?

Creating a Caring Culture through Inclusive Policies

This includes what the organization builds into its ecosystem to enable leaders and individuals to apply care consistently over time and across geographies. It also reinforces the values and priorities of the organization. The policies that it puts in place are an important factor in cultivating a caring environment.

For example, let's take a policy such as flexible working and the diversity of needs which this could benefit in a multicultural and demographically diverse workforce. Many times, it is not just the policy itself, but also how it is worded, that could unintentionally exclude certain groups of people. For instance, until recent years, maternity and paternity leave benefits were defined specifically to birthing parents only—but what if the couple is adopting or has used a surrogate (where it is locally legal)? How can policies use language which includes everyone regardless of gender, sexual orientation, or family type? Policy making is complex and needs thoughtful consideration and extensive engagement for it to be successfully adopted. The act of engagement itself also indicates inclusion.

Workplace accessibility is another big challenge that has to be addressed at an organizational level. Earlier in the book, I highlighted the barriers that can exist in the workplace. How does your organization approach accessibility? Is this even something you've considered before?

The benefit of removing barriers by considering the experiences of the people with disabilities and their challenges at work is that the changes made will more than likely benefit everyone else and create more awareness about workplace standards and the importance of ensuring accessibility for all.

However, policies are only as good as the leaders who implement them and reinforce how they are used. It is the mindsets and behaviours which bring about lasting change.

Be Intentional in How You Show Up

Mental health and well-being are also topics that have become important in the workplace. Even though we may have the best of intentions, it can sometimes be difficult to know the best way to discuss if someone's mental ill health has resulted in poor work performance, or if it is work related stress that has resulted in mental ill health and poor performance. These are nuanced discussions that call for sensitivity.

But as leaders, we need to be prepared for these conversations as the majority of us will experience mental ill health, either directly or indirectly, during our lifetimes. One in four people in the world will be affected by a mental or neurological disorder at some point in their lives. According to the World Health Organization, in 2021, more than three billion people worldwide were living with a neurological condition.[20] That makes neurological conditions the leading cause of ill health and disability globally. What's more, one in eight people in the world live with a mental health disorder—

[20] World Health Organization: WHO (2024) *Over 1 in 3 people affected by neurological conditions, the leading cause of illness and disability worldwide*. Available at: https://www.who.int/news/item/14-03-2024-over-1-in-3-people-affected-by-neurological-conditions--the-leading-cause-of-illness-and-disability-worldwide.

that equates to 970 million people.[21] However, many do not seek help due to the stigma associated with mental illness and mental disorders. Governments and organizations alike have a part to play to break this vicious cycle and to address the stigma associated with mental illness.

Mental health disorders include anxiety and depression, and the reality is that this isn't a 'future problem' for many of us, it's one we're living and experiencing now.

One aspect of workplace inclusion that can help with this is care and psychological safety so that employees who seek support can come forward without fear of being penalized. It is now common to see initiatives such as, 'It's okay to not be okay' in organizations, which seek to destigmatize mental illness and create a workplace where it is okay to reach out and say, 'I'm not okay.' Ultimately, we can only give our best at work if we are well both physically and mentally.

Understanding Our Impact

The benefit of building resilience into an organization is that it provides that common ground and support for everyone to be at their best for themselves and others at work.

Before the Covid-19 pandemic, many leaders struggled a bit more than they do today to understand the level of

[21] World Health Organization: WHO (2022) *Mental disorders*. Available at: https://www.who.int/news-room/fact-sheets/detail/mental-disorders.

influence they could have in supporting others in the area of mental well-being. The topic of mental well-being came to the forefront of all of our minds, with many of us having a much closer view and experience of physical and mental ill health, or even becoming caregivers for others who were suffering. Leaders were having to make decisions to protect the health of their staff and loved ones. Many times, they didn't have time to overthink and were making decisions based on their values and the shared values across the organization.

Although the Covid-19 lockdowns may be behind us, there is one challenge to employee well-being that is common across all industries and organizations—burnout. This is a theme Simon has also noticed in his work, where he's seen burnout coming up in conversation in industries as diverse as hospitality, creative agencies, and education.

'I started wondering why burnout is so prevalent and I think one possible reason is because of the fast-paced, connected world we live in.

'It used to take days for "snail mail" to reach us. Perhaps if you had access to a fax machine, you could get correspondence more quickly. But the bottom line was that as soon as you stepped out of the office, you weren't contactable. There was a very clear boundary between work and home. When you were at home, you could spend time with your family. When you were at work, you worked. But now, everyone is very connected.

Even if you don't reply to work emails on days off or in the evenings, that doesn't mean you don't see the notification on your phone. That in itself can be triggering for some people.

'Organizations want to improve the work experience as they recognize that staff who are burned out do not show up at their best. Not only does this affect the company's bottom line, but it also affects staff morale among the rest of that team.

'More leaders care about the well-being of their teams now than ever before, because they can see there is a tangible link to individual, team, and organizational performance outcomes. What I've noticed is that the most effective investments target three levels: individual, leaders, and the organization's culture. When it can align around well-being on these three levels, they are better able to sustain such initiatives and bring out the best in their people.'

As Simon says, well-being initiatives can be highly beneficial to everyone at an organization, but it's essential that senior leaders bring their curiosity to the table when discussing mental health and how to improve it. The growing awareness around burnout and its causes is positive, but we have to focus on the positive aspects of well-being, as well as solving the challenges presented by mental ill health. Ask yourself: How can you start an open and honest conversation about well-being in your organization? Are there any difficult topics you need to discuss? Why do you feel those conversations might be challenging?

Fighting the Fear

A common reason I am given for people not doing more around inclusion, or for not intervening, is the fear of saying or doing the wrong thing. This is particularly the case among leaders, when it comes to engaging with people who aren't their direct reports.

They hesitate about asking someone how they're feeling. They worry that they may have misinterpreted something and that by asking if the other person is okay, they'll somehow offend them. But I believe the way to reduce the risk of 'saying the wrong thing' is to show some vulnerability yourself.

So, let's imagine you've noticed that one of your colleagues seems to be a little quieter than usual and isn't engaging in conversations as much as normal. They aren't your direct report, and you're a couple of levels of leadership above them. You can reach out and say, 'Hey, how are you doing? I noticed that you aren't engaging as much as normal, is everything okay?'

By asking the question and opening up the conversation, you've shown that you've cared to notice and to check-in. If the other person told you they were fine, when in reality they're not, you may have helped them to feel safe enough to discuss it with someone else in the organization. Or maybe, they will reflect and come back to the conversation with you at a later time.

The key to getting this right more than getting it wrong is to show empathy, and to be ready to course correct and show curiosity and humility if you do get it wrong.

I was recently in the office when one of my colleagues caught me and introduced me to his line manager who had been on a work trip to various countries. When I said hello and introduced myself, I got a half-hearted smile in return. He looked tired. Without thinking, I said, 'You look tired.'

Of course, that was the wrong thing to say, especially to someone I'd only just met! I immediately caught myself, 'I'm so sorry, that was a horrible way to welcome you! I'm sorry if I offended you.' It was quite embarrassing to feel I needed to apologize after less than a minute of conversation, but I didn't want him to think that the only thing I'd noticed about him was that he looked tired. My initial comment about his appearance came from a place of care, but he wouldn't necessarily have known that.

The point is, we're all human. We won't get it right all the time. I'm sure all of us have been on the receiving end of a funny comment, or someone who's accidentally said the wrong thing without thinking. If the intent behind the comment comes from the right place, it's much easier to apologize for the mistake and move past it.

That said, I'm sure we've all also been on the receiving end of someone showing that they really care about us, and therefore we know how much of a difference that can make when we're not feeling okay.

Tiny Rice Grains Contemplation

Explore: Are you happy with your own level of self-care? If yes, why? If you're not, why not? What could you do differently?

Unpack: When was the last time you asked someone else at work if they were okay? What was the outcome? How might you approach that conversation differently next time?

Your reflections:

Know

....

....

Feel

....

....

Do

....

....

Chapter 9

Kindness and Humanity in Leadership

Terminologies like 'care' and 'kindness' are often described as being 'soft language' in a business context but take a moment to consider these questions. Do you want to create a work culture where everyone feels respected, valued, and can contribute to the business outcomes? In terms of safety, do you want the people at your organization to call out any dangers or hazards they see without fear of being penalized? If the answer to both those questions is a yes, then you want to embed care and kindness in your organization.

In the last chapter, we explored the importance of caring for ourselves, and also for showing kindness to ourselves. I'd like to dive a little deeper into kindness in particular in this chapter. Perhaps, take a moment now to ask yourself how you show care and kindness to those in your life.

When work gets busy, it is perhaps easy to forget about the 'nice' things like being kind and, instead, just focus on getting work done. But the thing is, these are both not mutually exclusive. We can be kind, show care, but also get work done.

As we discussed in the previous chapter with Simon, burnout is a global problem and one that often leads to people taking time out of work. What if kindness could help us combat that problem? This is not such a far-fetched idea. Research shows that kindness not only increases our self-esteem, empathy, and compassion, but that it also improves our mood and lowers both our blood pressure and the levels of the stress hormone cortisol in our bodies.[22]

In short, kindness makes us healthier.

Kindness also increases our sense of connectivity to those around us, and decreases our feelings of loneliness. In Chapter 2, I shared with you some of Matthew Lieberman's research about the pain of social exclusion, and how this feels just as uncomfortable as physical pain. What if a bit of kindness meant we all felt more connected, and therefore less lonely?

One thing that I have noticed, however, is that it is very difficult to give kindness unless you have experienced kindness yourself. I think if you asked any organization if they'd like to have a healthier workforce, the answer would be a yes. So, to my mind, the real question then is, what does kindness cost

---

[22] LPC, S.S.Psy.D. (2023) *The art of kindness*. Available at: https://www.mayoclinichealthsystem.org/hometown-health/speaking-of-health/the-art-of-kindness

you? What can you do to focus on bringing more kindness into your life, and the lives of those around you?

Embracing Kindness to Self

I know that everything we have talked about in this book so far can feel like a lot to ask for, so this is a good reminder to be kind to yourself. This is a journey. There might be times when you make mistakes, but there will also be times when you have made a huge impact. You have to find a way to step back, see the bigger picture and show yourself some kindness and recognition for all the effort you are putting in to move the needle on DEI. This is especially important when we notice that we have negative self-talk, it is in these moments where we need kindness the most.

Jane told us that she asks herself, 'What's my well-being state?' when she feels she is not at her best. What questions can you ask yourself to check in? Are you discouraged? What do you need to do to get into a better space? How can you support yourself?

How to Show Kindness to Yourself

I am definitely not an expert, and this is a tricky topic, because how we show kindness to ourselves varies from person to person. All I can do is share some of the ways in which I show kindness to myself, and hope that you find some of them useful.

About a year ago, I started a simple meditation habit to develop and practise mindfulness. One of my favourite mindfulness practices to start my day is the 'loving kindness' meditation. What I have noticed is that, even in such a state, it is much harder to contemplate loving kindness towards myself than it is towards others.

I found this completely surprising and it got me to reflect on why that was the case. I've always thought I was pretty kind to myself and that I take care of my physical and mental well-being. So, what was missing?

Through deeper reflection, I have come to appreciate that in addition to my self-care habits, kindness to self is about integrating various elements into my life to cultivate a more compassionate relationship with myself. Many of these areas are about 'being' rather than 'doing'.

Here I share how I am practising *being* more mindful of the way I interact with myself, because it impacts how I interact with others:

1. *Being realistic:* Setting goals that are challenging but are also attainable, avoiding setting standards that are too high and unrealistic.
2. *Practising self-compassion:* Allowing myself to make mistakes and treating myself with understanding and forgiveness rather than harsh criticism.

3. *Prioritizing self-care:* Making time for activities that nourish my physical, mental, and emotional well-being, such as exercise, relaxation, and hobbies.
4. *Setting boundaries:* Knowing my limits and being assertive in saying no to things that overwhelm or drain me, even if it means disappointing others.
5. *Celebrating achievements:* Acknowledging my accomplishments, no matter how small, and celebrating progress along the way.
6. *Seeking support:* Being willing to ask for help when needed and surrounding myself with people who uplift and encourage me.

In being mindful of these elements and integrating them into my life, is about finding acceptance of where I am in the present moment. So, how can you show kindness to yourself and reflect this kindness to others around you because of how you show up?

Becoming More Present

I have found that meditation is a great tool for becoming more present. I'm not going to get into how to meditate on a practical level in this book. There are many resources available, if you want to learn some techniques. What I'd like to explore, however, is how kindness and being present lead to connection with ourselves and with others.

Our brains are wired to be social and to have connections. When we can bring our awareness inwards and connect to ourselves, it makes our connections to others stronger.

Becoming more present can benefit all of us, regardless of the level at which we work. In the book, *Mindfulness at Work*, Dr Stephen McKenzie reveals how the practice of mindfulness, which is our ability to focus on what is versus being distracted by what isn't, can help manage stress at work.[23]

When we are frequently in a rush we tend to feel flustered and a little bit out of control, whereas if we take a moment for ourselves before we start the day the physiological impact of slowing down and taking a breath is that we feel more grounded and composed.

Take a moment now to notice who you are, where you are, and what you're doing. How often do you do that before rushing into a task, or getting started with your working day? I'm sure all of us have been told to, 'Take a breather and slow down,' at some point in our lives.

But do we always do it?

Running on Empty

Earlier in the book, I shared that I was diagnosed with the mood disorder hypomania in 2009. This means I always have to be

---

[23] McKenzie, S. (2013) *Mindfulness at work: How to Avoid Stress, Achieve More and Enjoy Life!* Exisle Publishing.

watchful about doing too much, and how that plays out for me. Although I have got better at managing myself and knowing when to stop, it doesn't mean it's any easier to do so.

I have learned from experience that it is better to slow down sometimes, than to keep racing ahead. I decided to press pause in 2023. I took a two-month sabbatical, because I was on the verge of burnout. I could have gone on at work, albeit with a lot of difficulty, but I took the decision to slow things down. I had reached a stage in my life when I was asking myself, 'What's next?' I had many thoughts running around in my head about my job and the impact I wanted to create, as well as about my personal life. All of that meant just getting on with the day felt overwhelming each morning.

I was very easily distracted. Even reading a page of a book was too much for my mind. Everything felt like it was taking me double the effort it used to. So, I hit the pause button. For the first few days, I just slept. I was mentally exhausted. I know this isn't uncommon, as many other people who feel the need to take a pause have told me they feel the same. I knew I wanted to find a way out of this burnout that was kinder to myself, but also something I could practise.

This was what led me to active mindfulness, because I thought this might be able to help me slow down and quieten my mind. I was already attending a mindfulness course, which helped me learn new skills for being present. But my sabbatical also gave me time to do other things that I had been neglecting in my life, such as spending more time with my daughter before her wedding and just dealing with the many personal demands that fill up our lives.

When I slowed down, I realized that, even without work, I had a very full life. About four weeks into my sabbatical, I paused and realized I was about to speed off to a tennis class, then meet someone for lunch, and at the back of my mind, I was considering whether I should write this book, and I was managing a small renovation at home. I thought, 'How did I fit this around work?' It felt like I was two people doing all of these things. No wonder I was running on empty every morning before I even got out of bed.

This pause gave me an opportunity to look at everything I was doing and make some choices around what I should prioritize and what I would need to give up. I had to learn to set boundaries. It helped me realize that there were many things I was doing each week out of habit, not because I really enjoyed them.

This feeling of being rushed, stretched, and being everything to everyone is not unique to me. As leaders, especially, we can carry so much accountability not only for ourselves, but also for others that we almost feel as though we can't stop because something is going to give. But here's the challenge: If we don't stop, something will give anyway. If I hadn't stopped when I did, something would have given and it would have taken me longer than two months to get back to what I wanted to prioritize, and it would likely have had a bigger impact on other people too. I may as well have needed to be away from work for longer. In my personal life, the people I love and care about would have been impacted by me not being my best self.

My ability to hit pause was fortuitous, but it was no accident that I was able to notice my own triggers and take the decision to have some time out. As well as being able to recognize for myself that I needed a break, I also had the support of leaders, colleagues, family, and friends.

Perhaps, take a moment here to reflect on how you feel each day. Are you exhausted before you even start? Do you feel as though your to-do list is overwhelmingly long? What would it take for you to hit the pause button? What might that space and time give you?

I believe that the next generation of leaders understand this concept of slowing down better than those who have gone before them. However, their challenge is the many distractions in the digital world, particularly from technology and information coming from so many directions, that meant it can be hard to take that time to slow down.

I'm not the only one. Simon has also focused his attention on helping young people develop the skills they'll need throughout their lives to show kindness to themselves and look after their own well-being.

'We currently offer programmes with the Happiness Institute to children from seven years old, because we realized that our beliefs and how we see the world come from our caregivers and our early life experiences. We thought there was no better time to start helping people build resilience than from a young age, before they get to teenage, where things can get very challenging for them.

'We now work with school children, teachers, and parents to help promote positive behaviours for well-being. The world children grow up in is very different to what my generation experienced. Nowadays, the technology and gadgets available make things harder. For example, bullying is something that happens to many of us when we're young—within school groups, we are often either bullied or become bullies. But when I was growing up, someone could only be bullied when they were physically present. If someone bullied you, it was easier to simply avoid being in the same place as them.

'But now, children are living in a digital world, and they're being bullied in that digital world. It's incessant and it can be very pervasive. One of the ways in which we've been working to combat this is through well-being circles. These are run for the community, by volunteers, to help people learn well-being skills. We normally have five or six children per group, who have been selected by their schools, because they are exhibiting some signs of being at high risk of mental ill health—that might be through their behaviour, or the way they socialize with others.

'My biggest joy is that their teachers tell us that they can see a change in their behaviour. Over the course of eight to ten sessions, the teachers tell us that these children have more brightness in their eyes. They exhibit more prosocial behaviour, show more gratefulness to their teacher, and show more kindness to their friends. The outcome we hope to achieve with these well-being circles is for each child to see the best versions of themselves, and work towards becoming them. One of the activities we have them do is to draw their best possible self and set small goals towards achieving that.'

What a wonderful way to get children to engage with well-being. But what can we adults learn from this approach? Do you know what the best version of yourself could look like? Are there any steps you can take to help you become that person?

Acts of Kindness

Performing an act of kindness means harbouring a spirit of helpfulness, as well as being generous and considerate, without expecting anything in return. When you frame acts of kindness like that, can you think of an example from the last week where you performed an act of kindness, or maybe you have been the recipient of an act of kindness?

In workplaces where acts of kindness are the norm, the effects can multiply fast. Research shows that when people receive one, they pay it back not only to the same person, but often to someone entirely new.[24] It's another example of a positive ripple effect that one action can have. This leads to a culture of generosity in an organization—and it's one that I've seen myself in my time at Shell.

There is a building resilience module titled 'Random Acts of Kindness', which is one of my favourite sessions to facilitate. I start by asking everyone to share one thing they've done that day or that week, which could be called a random act of kindness. What I find interesting is that every time I run this session, I see people let their guards down as soon as they start to share and the whole mood in the room changes. There's more softness, empathy, goodwill, and a spirit of sharing. This was one of the things that got me thinking about the power of kindness.

The other was the burnout epidemic, which Simon and I discussed in the previous chapter. More and more people and businesses are looking for a way through burnout and I believe kindness is an important element in building resilience. However, kindness isn't a 'skill' you can teach so much as a quality you can embody, I believe we can all focus on being

---

[24] Hanley-Dafoe R., (2023) *Why Kindness Matters*. Available at: https://www.psychologytoday.com/gb/blog/everyday-resilience/202303/the-remarkable-power-of-kindness-and-why-it-matters

kind to ourselves, first and foremost, and acting with kindness towards others.

The beauty of random acts of kindness is that they can be very small—but much like our tiny grains of rice, each grain has a hardiness and character of its own and when they are put together, this strength multiplies into something much greater than the sum of its parts. Random acts of kindness happen all around us. It's the time you're at the grocery store and realize you're just a few cents short for your shopping, and someone in the queue behind you gives you the change you need. It's helping someone carry a heavy shopping bag. It's holding a door open for the person behind you.

We can each cultivate an attitude where we tell ourselves that we will show more empathy or be more compassionate each day, and in doing so, the acts of kindness will naturally follow. How can you build some time into the start of your day to be mindful and focus on being kind? How do you want to behave towards yourself and others?

Creating an Ecosystem of Kindness

Kindness is the foundation on which we build networks as humans. You could even say kindness is the foundation for humanity. Throughout this book, we've talked a lot about what leaders can give, but what can leaders receive? Rather than thinking of kindness as something you simply give out or spread for others, I invite you to think of kindness as an ecosystem that underpins your networks and relationships.

None of us can do this work around DEI alone. This is work that will need to continue long after we've left the workforce. We all need support, and through the leaders I've worked with, I've learned the best way to generate that support is to show kindness to others and welcome it in return.

Think for a moment about the strong and lasting relationships you have in your life, whether at work or personally. What is required for any relationship to give you the sense of inclusion and belonging that makes it feel like a safe, supportive partnership? I imagine kindness and empathy are among the things you thought of.

How can we form strong and empathetic relationships with our colleagues? The answer, I believe, is to approach those relationships with kindness and a sense of [non-romantic] love. Love can touch us on many levels. We can talk about our love for the organization we work for and the work it is doing, or perhaps, love for the culture that you've created and want to sustain.

Standing Out as a Leader for DEI

Throughout this book, I have discussed and provided stories and examples of those who have set themselves apart as

DEI leaders, regardless of their job title. The first way in which they do this is through their values and intentions. The second is how they show up. When I started my role at Shell, for the first time my daughters didn't ask me what I 'did' at work, because it was visible that I was advocating for DEI.

I remember coming out of one of my earliest meetings with the enABLE group, who are the ERG around disability inclusion at Shell, and bursting into tears. I'd gone into that meeting with my plans for what we were going to do, and within five minutes of me starting to talk, all I'd heard were a list of dozens of things that just didn't work. I felt shattered and when I left that meeting, I thought, 'How am I even going to get started?'

My daughter also saw how nervous I was while talking about the areas related to LGBTQ+ inclusion. But you are a leader in DEI when you start showing up in these areas and look for ways to make things better, even if doing so makes you feel uncomfortable. I've found that it's when you become uncomfortable that you really learn.

And finally, what will set you apart as a leader in DEI is being able to laugh at yourself, because there will be occasions when you will put your foot in your mouth.

I remember attending a conference by the Business Disability Forum in London in 2019. It was to launch a study which my organization had sponsored called 'Towards a Disability Smart

World: Developing a Global Disability Inclusion Strategy'[25] and I was there as the global head of DEI. During one of the coffee breaks, another attendee standing in the line asked me where the milk was. I pointed to the jug a little further down the table without thinking twice.

But then, I saw one of the waiters reach over, get the jug, and put it in front of the person who'd asked me for the same. He said, 'It's right here in front of you on the table, would you like me to add some to your coffee?' I caught the waiter's eye and that was when I realized: the person who'd asked me was visually impaired. Of course, I felt embarrassed, but the moment had passed. They had their coffee, I got mine. But it's a valuable lesson that no matter how much work we do on ourselves, we can still trip, even when we have the best of intentions.

But it's Donny Ching who, perhaps, put it best when it comes to what being a leader, whether in DEI or any other part of business, really looks like.

'I think as a leader, your biggest responsibility is to unleash talent. When you demonstrate kindness and take a personal interest, which I mean in a holistic sense, to those around you, you will start to notice a difference. People will begin to feel

---

[25] *New research reveals strategies for global disability inclusion* (2020). Available at: https://businessdisabilityforum.org.uk/news-opinion/press-release-new-research-reveals-strategies-for-global-disability-inclusion/.

more empowered. They'll have more courage and feel free to speak more openly, and to push and challenge.

'One of the questions I asked myself throughout my career was, how do I level the playing field? This is a question any of us can ask ourselves, at any time. I think empathetic leadership is sometimes missing in the workplace nowadays, and kindness is often considered a weakness. But I believe empathy and kindness are our superpowers as leaders. Most people tell you that they want a human leader, so how can we embody these traits and deliver that for them?'

Tiny Rice Grains Contemplation

Explore: What does kindness mean to you, both personally and in the context of your work?

Unpack: What can you do to focus on bringing more kindness into your life, and the lives of those around you? How can you embody being more human as a leader by activating the leadership superpowers of empathy and kindness?

Your reflections:

Know

....

....

Feel

....

....

Do

....

....

Conclusion

If you've read this book cover to cover, it might seem that I'm asking a lot of you—especially if this is all new to you. My intention is not to suggest that we should all be applying all of these actions, all of the time, but to share my and others' experiences, to help you navigate your own DEI journey.

Sometimes, you will need to find the courage to be vulnerable, or to change the status quo. Other days, you might be called on to be more curious, to ask what don't I see? What do I need to learn? But if you take only one thing from these pages, I hope it is the power of kindness. If you don't know where to begin, start by asking, what can I do to be kinder to myself? Then, go from there. It's remarkable how showing a little kindness to yourself can radiate out into the world.

Take time on this journey to use this book however suits you. Read the chapters in any order you please, dip in and out of them.

As you do so, I suggest that you *consistently reflect on the following*:

1. How do you want to show up for yourself and your team? How can you use courage, curiosity, and care to guide you in creating an inclusive workplace culture?
2. What resonates with you and serves as an inspiration for you to be bold and drive change, even when it is uncomfortable?
3. How will you make space to focus on DEI in the way you lead and the way you work? How will you hold yourself and your team(s) accountable for inclusion?

The 'Tiny Rice Grains Contemplation' at the end of each chapter is an additional opportunity to dive deeper and to give yourself time to pause and reflect.

Before we finish, let's come back to the concept of our tiny rice grains. In the Preface, Girish eloquently shared what tiny rice grains mean in Indian culture, and how this relates to DEI. I loved what he shared on many levels. Firstly, that just a few grains of rice—in our case, the importance we place on DEI—is enough for each of us to add value to this world and make it a more inclusive place. Secondly, that the nourishment rice provides and the care with which it is prepared speaks to the wholehearted care we need to take to help everyone bring their best selves to work and feel safe doing so. Thirdly, if we get our staple food—such as rice—right then, all the rest of the side dishes fall into place alongside it. DEI is the staple in our context, with language, nationality, culture, and many other factors making up our side dishes. And finally, that being willing to share a few grains of rice—or our wholehearted care and kindness—with others is a sign of globalized thinking that will ripple out into the world and make it a better place for all.

On their own, each of our tiny rice grains may not seem like they amount to much, but together, they have more power and potential than we perhaps realize. So, share your tiny rice grains with kindness and begin changing the world, one conversation and action at a time.

If you'd like to explore further and discuss anything we've covered in this book, or about DEI more generally, please reach out to me via my LinkedIn, I'd love to hear from you.

https://www.linkedin.com/in/lyn-lee-dei/

Acknowledgements

To my two beautiful daughters, Clare and Val, the talented young women who show so much generosity, kindness, and compassion, and with a strong sense of right and wrong. Thank you for putting up with Mummy, and for being the adult in our mother-daughter relationship, for being my conscience, my worst critic, but also my strongest supporter. Your strength is my inspiration and I am very proud of you both.

To my furkids Averell, Bailey, Fuji, Ella, Everest, and Mooey (and my four ninja turtles). You bring so much joy, chaos, and randomness into my life. Thank you for the laughter you bring. You are my dose of sunshine when life throws a curveball.

To my friends and leaders: Simon Leow, Sherman Ho, Ashana Heera, Girish K., Olga Kortbeek, Jason Romero, Vishal Kumar, Kelvin Gee, Asada Harinsuit, Carlos Maurer, Jane Low, Kevin Smith, Michael Massey, Dustin Henry, Lara Magat, Donny Ching, Ronan Cassidy, Cherrelle Williams, and all others who have chosen to remain anonymous. All of whom have so generously contributed their stories, time, and resources to this book: without your voices and support, there would not be this book.

And finally, to all the teams I've led and collaborated with and to the employee resource groups around the world. We've learned, laughed, cried together, and stood strongly together to deliver this work. It has not always been easy, but the journey has been made lighter and more meaningful because of having all of you by my side.

I am grateful.